The Transition

WINNING THE 4TH QUARTER OF LIFE

Dennis Niewoehner

Outskirts Press, Inc.
Denver, Colorado

The opinions expressed in this manuscript are solely the opinions of the author and do not represent the opinions or thoughts of the publisher. The author has represented and warranted full ownership and/or legal right to publish all the materials in this book.

The Transition
Winning the 4th Quarter of Life
All Rights Reserved.
Copyright © 2009 Dennis Niewoehner
V3.0

Cover Photo © 2009 Dennis Niewoehner. All rights reserved - used with permission.

This book may not be reproduced, transmitted, or stored in whole or in part by any means, including graphic, electronic, or mechanical without the express written consent of the publisher except in the case of brief quotations embodied in critical articles and reviews.

Outskirts Press, Inc.
http://www.outskirtspress.com

ISBN: 978-1-4327-1231-0

Library of Congress Control Number: 2009922195

Outskirts Press and the "OP" logo are trademarks belonging to Outskirts Press, Inc.

PRINTED IN THE UNITED STATES OF AMERICA

CONTENTS

Acknowledgments	v
Introduction	1
Chapter One *Financial Planning*	11
Chapter Two *Why the "Point of Transition" is so Important*	37
Chapter Three *To Transition is to Change*	43
Chapter Four *When Adversity Hits and Choices are Made*	51
Chapter Five *Everything is a Function of Attitude*	61
Chapter Six *Perseverance*	67
Chapter Seven *Organization and Goals – The Great Equalizers*	77
Chapter Eight *Your Best Health in the 4th Quarter*	89

Chapter Nine 113
Tax Planning

Chapter Ten 127
Estate Planning

Chapter Eleven 149
What Do I Do Now?

Journal 161
Adversity & Perseverance
(My Story About Four Years of Struggle)

Acknowledgments

First and foremost, I would like to thank my contributing authors for all the work and time they put into writing their specific chapters on financial planning, tax and estate planning, and health and wellness. Since each one of them is at the top of his respective field, I would be hard pressed to find four busier individuals. Dr. Larry Emmons is one of the top radiologists in Denver, Colorado and helps oversee the operations of Diversified Radiology of Colorado, a company comprised of over 150 employees, including 50 radiologists. It has been a distinct pleasure getting to know Larry while serving on the Parker Adventist Hospital Board together. David Twibell, President of Colorado Wealth Management, deserves a special thanks in that he found the time to write his chapter while managing millions of dollars for his clients during the current Financial Crisis. Last but not least are my two friends who are top legal professionals in Denver, Bill Gougér and Michael Franzmann. Their law firm, Gougér Franzmann & Hooke, LLC is highly respected in Denver regarding tax and estate matters.

A special thanks is also due two people who are not only partners at Ryden & Associates but also husband and wife. Jerome and Su Ryden went beyond the call of duty assisting me with still photography shots and video production for my promotional DVD. Like the others, they are very busy people. As a matter of fact, while assisting me, Su was running for the Colorado House of Representatives. I am happy to report that she was successful and won her seat. I also want to extend my thanks to Bart Bacon of Bacon Designs for professionally designing and producing my website.

A special debt of gratitude is due my assistant, Kristi Schneider, for her assistance from the earliest draft of my manuscript to the final product. Her critiques, although sometimes without mercy, always had the success of the book in mind. I also had the pleasure of working with Kristi's daughter, Samantha Schneider, who was one of my earliest editors, as well as Kristi's sister, Jeanne McGrain, who provided the final editing work.

Throughout the entire process I had the encouragement and support of my wife, Marcia. Not only did I receive her praise for the product itself, but also for wanting to help others in the 4th quarter of life. When I am on a mission I am known to be a workaholic who devotes many personal hours to accomplish my goals. For this, I thank her for her patience.

Introduction

    Late in the summer of 2008, I had just completed writing this book when the national Financial Crisis hit Wall Street and all across America. I had already copyrighted the manuscript and sent a number of manuscript copies out to publishers in New York.
    Although I had worked long and hard getting the book to this stage, there was no doubt I needed to rewrite it to address how the Financial Crisis was going to affect we Baby Boomers heading towards our retirement years. The financial world as we knew it had just been turned upside down. This crisis will affect everyone, especially those of us in our 50s and 60s approaching retirement who don't have the luxury of time to return lost value to our portfolios. We are feeling the impact of the Financial Crisis

The Transition

in that the value of our homes, retirement plans and nest eggs have severely declined. We have lost nearly a decade of stock growth and real estate appreciation.

After rewriting the manuscript to provide information regarding the effects of the Financial Crisis on the Baby Boomers, I feel this book will be of more help now than ever before. To transition into the 4th quarter of life is difficult enough, but to be simultaneously subjected to both the crumbling world economy as well as your own investments is monumental. This situation, however, must be dealt with. Age cannot be put on hold, waiting for a more convenient time, so we must still make a smooth transition into the 4th quarter while we deal with the affects of the financial crisis. It is more important than ever before to know how to deal with financial, lifestyle and age-related changes.

With all of the new financial burdens facing the Baby Boomers, my chapters on adversity, perseverance, hope and how to make choices are even more applicable. In addition, friends of mine, one who is a financial manager and two who are attorneys, discuss financial, tax and estate issues. I have always enjoyed and adhered to the quote, "When wealth is lost, something is lost. When health is lost, all is lost." As a believer of this quote, I have asked a doctor to address health and wellness issues that face we Baby Boomers.

When trying to understand and deal with financial issues, many of us head to our local book store. When I have done so, I've noticed that most of the books on the shelves are written by financial planners who tell us <u>what to do</u> but don't tell us <u>how to handle</u> the adversity itself so that success can be achieved. I also noticed that many of these books are written by professional writers such as teachers and well-known speakers, and are typically written by the younger

Introduction

generation or those people who have made a career of teaching but not actually doing. The bottom line is that they are very good at giving advice but typically have not had first-hand experience in solving life's real problems, i.e. they talk the talk but have not walked the walk. If you are like me, you listen more to those you can identify with, who actually are going through similar experiences, as well as those who have had real life experience.

Why do I feel qualified to assist my readers with transitioning and financial crisis problems? First of all, I just turned 63 and have been transitioning into the 4th quarter for the past several years. Being this age has helped me understand the transitioning process, as well as the trials and tribulations attributed to it. Besides being 63, the other reason I feel qualified to assist my readers with their transition and financial problems is that I have been in the financial and real estate industries for the past 35 years.

Earlier I mentioned that it is not only important to know what to do but how to handle the adversity itself so you can achieve success. Much of the advice given in this book comes from my personal experiences with the collapse of the Savings and Loan Industry in 1987 – 1991. This collapse had been the most serious financial crisis in the United States since the Great Depression. Different than now, most Americans were not directly affected by the fallout from the collapse, and since it has been over 20 years ago many people, including the Baby Boomers, do not remember the severity. In 2008, less than 25 banks have gone belly up. It has been predicted that about 3% of the nation's 8,500 federally-insured lenders won't survive. In comparison, during the collapse of the Savings and Loan Industry approximately 8% or 1,109 banks went out of business between 1987 and 1992. I guarantee you that I "walked the walk" in that I spent those four years being a warrior in my

The Transition

struggle to save my financial and emotional life. During this period I was fortunate enough to have kept a journal which I will share (located after Chapter11), and show how you too can fight through periods of extreme adversity.

Most everyone in America has heard the terms "credit crunch" and "financial crisis" but I believe only a few people really understand exactly what the situation is and how it happened. While I will let the financial experts comment regarding the details, I would like to provide a few of my own comments on what I feel happened and why. I will do this not from the level of a Wall Street investment banker, but from a more simple and philosophical level. Simply put, we were a nation that was out of control. As history has shown us, this has happened to other nations when their governments and people ignore and/or break the basic principles in life. We were operating under the principle of greed by being financially irresponsible and lowering our regulatory standards. The U.S. Government, in order to create growth in the economy, decreased its regulatory control in lending standards. The advent of sub-prime mortgages along with low interest rates enabled more people to buy homes than ever before. With more people buying homes, housing prices sky-rocketed as more people chased a limited supply of homes. Without adequate regulation in the mortgage industry, mortgage brokers and Wall Street financial institutions were able to be financially greedy by packaging these mortgages with thousands of other mortgages and then sell them, chopped up, as mortgage-backed securities to other financial institutions. Since so many mortgages had been made to borrowers who were not credit worthy, the payment terms could not be sustained by many of the borrowers. As more and more mortgages defaulted, not only did the housing market begin to collapse but all of the

Introduction

securitized mortgages sold to different institutions also came apart.

The lack of responsibility came, not only from the mortgage brokers and financial institutions, but also from existing homeowners themselves. As home prices increased, they borrowed heavily against their home equity in an attempt to raise their standard of living without making additional income. I believe it is best said by Alicia Munnel of Boston College's Center for Retirement Research, "The evidence suggests that the housing boom caused people to increase their borrowing, to extract equity from their homes and to raise their level of spending. The Federal Reserve Flow of Funds report shows total household debt...soaring to 120% of income in 2007 (from 80% in the 1990s). Most of this debt is home mortgage debt. Essentially, the result was that people had more debt. If they had kept all the cash they took out, they would be even. But they spent a third of the cash, so they are less well-off." She goes on to add, "For people approaching retirement, ages 50 to 62, we found that their net worth was 14% lower than it would have been without the housing boom."

Why did this happen? Why is it still out of control? Credit is the life blood of the U.S. economy. Without credit being available, the economy has severely slowed and those businesses which depend on credit have had to scale back or stop their day-to-day operations. This is also happening to the consumer. They have found themselves in too much debt without new credit being available to sustain their lifestyle. What has happened over time is that our national economy now works better when people spend and use debt, versus using their disposable income to create savings accounts and pay off existing debt. Even though spending and "consumer consumption" make our economy

The Transition

work, people using credit (too much), including leveraging their homes to buy consumer goods, actually fueled the beginning of the credit crisis.

I feel what has happened was very necessary in order to restore the basic principles of free enterprise as the United States has always known it, however I am less than pleased by who has to take the arrow in the chest. It isn't those on Wall Street who practiced greed nor is it those who borrowed too much on their credit cards or on housing they could not afford. It is those of us who for years have been financially responsible by purchasing our homes with cash down payments, investing our extra money into savings and/or equities and paying our taxes as required. Just to remind everyone, the government's financial bailout program is being funded by those of us who pay taxes.

I feel it will be the Baby Boomers who will be taking a triple hit. First of all, our equity in our housing and 401k investments has taken a severe loss in value. The time needed to recover these retirement equities is limited. Last but not least, and something not spoken of often, is that I feel the only way the government is going to get their trillions back from the bailout program is through higher taxes and future high inflation.

WHAT TO DO – MY RECOMMENDATIONS

    A. Protect Your Assets
    B. Prepare For Inflation

As I stated earlier, this book is primarily about <u>how to deal</u> with the negative situation and how we react to it as opposed to <u>what to do</u> financially. Again, we will let the financial advisors get into the specifics of what to do.

Introduction

However, with that being said, I still feel the two most important items to base your financial program and attitude on are to make sure all your plans revolve around protecting your assets, and preparing for future inflation. This should be the basis of your plan. A person with a plan doesn't drift (drifting causes panic.) Along with having to face and overcome adversities caused by this market meltdown, you are going to be forced to make some tough choices. In order to keep a positive attitude, let's call these choices nothing more than "adjustments to your original plans." For some people, these adjustments may have very severe consequences such as abandoning the idea of retirement altogether. For others, it may be nothing more serious than not buying a new car or taking a vacation.

Everyone over 55 reading this book knows that the aging process does affect your outlook on life and on many actions taken or not taken. Typically we become a little more cautious and fearful about our future whether it is our jobs, health or longevity. Many of us actually become more hesitant to take action and make changes in our lives; however, based upon my advice to take the proper steps to protect your assets and prepare for inflation, there are two things I would like you to do before anything else, and before meeting with your financial advisor. They are: 1) In your portfolio keep two years' worth of expenses on hand in liquid investments (money markets, certificates of deposit). Having cash on hand gives you a sense of control and can limit your losses in the future if the market continues to fall. 2) Continue to stay engaged in the investment process. In the past, stockbrokers and financial advisors have always advised not touching your stock or bond portfolio and waiting a number of years until they come back. They use

The Transition

the line that, until you sell a stock or a bond, you do not have a recorded loss...it is only a paper loss at the time. I have never agreed with this philosophy and this financial crisis is an event that America has never seen since 1929. After meeting with your financial advisor or stockbroker, sell the dogs in your portfolio that more than likely will never have a chance of recovery. This can create the cash that you need for security and also free up ready cash to take advantage of the market to upgrade into stocks and funds that are undervalued due to the market meltdown. I feel this investment philosophy not only helps protect your asset portfolio but prepares you for future inflation by having stock in companies which have a great future in front of them.

Lastly, I would like to offer my advice regarding what you should do about your declining home value. Even though you have lost equity you may have been counting on for retirement, do not do anything that takes your name off the deed to the house. In other words, do not sell your home. Even if you need to go back to work or work longer, do not sell your home. If possible, do not tap into your home's equity to create extra cash. This is especially true if you currently have a mortgage loan with a low interest rate. Your home is going to be one of the most important tools to fight future inflation. If I am correct in my premise that we are going to be experiencing high inflation, your home will rise in value as it has in other periods of inflation, creating additional net worth for your retirement.

Before the national Financial Crisis arrived in our lives, a chapter entitled "Financial Planning" by David Twibell, President of Colorado Wealth Management Company, appeared as Chapter Seven in this book. This chapter was to be a source of age-specific financial information to assist us in the transition process. This chapter, along with the

Introduction

chapters regarding tax planning, estate planning, and health and wellness issues were added to make this the most complete book on the market for discussing transition issues.

Now, with financial issues and concerns being at the forefront of everyone's minds, I have moved it to the front of the book as Chapter One. Another reason I felt it is better as Chapter One is because of an earlier statement that I made in this Introduction. It is the financial advisor's responsibility to advise us on the specifics of <u>what to do</u> in the financial planning process. As a result, it made total sense to read about <u>what to do</u> prior to discussing <u>how to cope</u> with these financial issues and the changes we are feeling as we transition into the 4th quarter of life. The financial crisis itself and how it affects us is monumental, but as you read this book and live your life, remember these important points:

1. Even though it is important to not put our assets at risk, it is more important to protect our happiness and not put that at risk.
2. We must remember how to focus on what is important in our lives.
3. We still have to take responsibility for our own future

Chapter One
Financial Planning

By David Twibell, J.D.

For the past 17 years I have had the pleasure of helping hundreds of people entering the 4th quarter of life, first as a practicing attorney and, more recently, as a wealth manager and investment advisor. These people have ranged from high-powered corporate executives to small business owners, and everyone in between.

I say this has been a pleasure because I truly believe that, when approached correctly, the 4th quarter can be the most exciting and rewarding part of life. I feel so strongly about this that I have spent the better part of the last five years speaking and writing on investment and planning topics that directly impact people entering this crucial part of their lives.

The Transition

I also have a different perspective on this issue beyond my involvement as a lawyer and financial advisor. I have seen first-hand the challenges facing people entering the 4th quarter as I have watched my father and mother transition into this period of their lives. I have been there as they have confronted and overcome many of the same challenges you are now facing. And through this experience, I believe I have learned as much if not more than I have in my nearly two decades of professional practice.

My hope is that through my professional and personal experiences working with people like you, I can help you overcome some of the challenges and avoid some of the mistakes that commonly confront people entering the 4th quarter of life.

You Are Ready For The 4th Quarter

Entering the 4th quarter of life can be a daunting financial prospect. You are likely transitioning from a relatively steady outside income stream to little or no outside income. You have probably shifted from saving and investing money for your retirement to worrying about whether you will have enough money available to meet your ongoing financial needs. And most importantly, you have likely reached a point where you can no longer afford to make major investment mistakes.

My goal in this chapter is to help you successfully confront these challenges. And I have some good news for you; you are already well-equipped to manage your financial affairs during the 4th quarter even if you may not realize it yet. After all, you have likely spent most of your life gaining knowledge and experience, learning to assess strengths and weaknesses, both in others and, more importantly, yourself.

Financial Planning

And believe it or not, these life experiences and the wisdom that only comes through making, and learning from, mistakes is far more valuable than any MBA, JD, or other degree or designation you could get.

What's Ahead?

The ancient Chinese philosopher Confucius is often credited with the proverb "may you live in interesting times." And while we can all agree the current environment is indeed "interesting," for many people entering the 4th quarter it is also fraught with danger and confusion.

For decades we have been told to save our money, invest wisely, and maintain a long-term outlook. If we did these things, we could expect our retirement savings to grow at a reasonable rate and, more importantly, we could expect it to be there when we needed it.

The current economic crisis casts these accepted principles into doubt. After all, many of you did exactly what you had been taught – work hard, live frugally, save, and invest wisely – only to have the rug pulled out from under you during the current crash.

The rules have now changed. During the rest of this chapter, I will examine how they have changed and what you need to do to safeguard and grow your investments as you enter the 4th quarter. Just as importantly, I will point out some of the common mistakes many people make and try to provide you with some tips on how to avoid them. Despite the recent economic crisis, I strongly believe that if you can overcome these common hurdles you will have a great start on the financial side of the 4th quarter.

The Transition

How The Crash of 2008 Changes The 4th Quarter

The current economic crisis will go down in the history books alongside some of the great economic disasters of our time. While not yet on a scale comparable with the Great Depression, it is likely that before the economy stabilizes we will have witnessed one of the most violent recessions of the past two centuries.

For many of you, the current economic crisis will force you to re-examine your investment assumptions and plans for the future. It is my hope that this chapter will provide you with the knowledge and tools necessary to successfully undertake this examination and prepare a new plan for you and your family.

What Happened And Why Didn't We See It Coming

One of the most frequent questions I am asked is how we got into this mess in the first place. After all, our financial institutions and government regulatory bodies are ostensibly manned by some of the best and brightest financial minds in the world. Why didn't they see this coming?

The sad truth is that many of them did. As recent congressional testimony shows, the warning signs of this impending economic collapse were apparent to many of our financial and government leaders. They understood that the era of cheap money, lax regulation and excessive risk could not last. The problem wasn't one of identification, but rather of will. Most of these same leaders owed much of their power, success, and wealth to the very mechanisms that threatened our future economic well-being. And when faced with a choice between their own pocketbooks and ours, guess who won.

Financial Planning

For the rest of us, we never had much of a chance. In retrospect, the warning signs of an impending economic collapse were there for us to see as well. The lack of transparency and systemic sleight-of-hand performed by Wall Street left us with the impression that things were far more stable than they actually were. Like passengers aboard the Titanic, we could see the tips of the icebergs but we couldn't guess how far below the surface they extended.

How You Can Get Back On Your Feet

For most investors, the reasons for the current economic crises are less important than where we go from here. After all, your goal now should be to figure out how to protect your portfolio in the years to come and, for many of you, how to recover the significant losses you have incurred.

New Plan For A New Environment. For most of the past 25 years, having a cogent investment strategy has been optional. After all, for many of you – particularly those who started investing in the booming 1980s and 1990s – your investment strategy was really limited to a decision about how much of your portfolio you should have invested in U.S. stocks and how much in U.S. bonds. When the markets climb nearly every year for almost two decades as they did from 1980 to 1999, investing is a pretty easy game.

Those types of basic allocation decisions simply won't cut it under the market conditions created by the 2008 Financial Crisis. As I discuss later in this chapter, simply buying good stocks and hanging onto them is not a sufficient strategy now. Instead, investors need a more comprehensive and customized plan for how they intend to

The Transition

navigate the 4th quarter.

So what is this new plan? Well, that really depends on you. I wish I could create a one-size-fits-all investment plan that would be useful to everyone reading this book. The truth is that I cannot.

Rather, I can help you design your own plan. And the first step in this process is for you to determine how much money you need and how much risk you are willing to take. These are two very basic questions, but they are overlooked by the vast majority of investors entering the 4th quarter.

The amount of money you need is a function of many things and is different for every person. Do you have a good grasp of your expenses going forward? Do you have health issues and, if so, do you have adequate insurance? Do you want to leave a legacy to your family or charity, or are you planning to spend the bulk of your retirement funds? These and myriad other questions are all relevant to how much money you actually need. And while some of these answers can be determined using a financial planning software program (or a good old-fashioned Excel spreadsheet), others are more philosophical in nature and may take several discussions with your spouse and family.

Regardless of the amount you actually decide upon, the next question will invariably be how much risk are you willing to take with your retirement funds in order to generate sufficient income and principal growth to see you through the 4th quarter. Again, this is a simple question with some potentially complex answers. In fact, the entire concept of risk has been thrown into disarray during the recent financial crisis as investors grapple with the changing nature of the financial markets. The bottom line, though, is that you will need to make an honest assessment of the amount of risk you are willing to take and ensure that your plan comports with this decision in order to develop a

Financial Planning

successful plan for the 4th quarter.

The final plank in your investment plan, and the one I will cover in much greater detail in the following section, is how to design an investment strategy that takes into account the threshold issues discussed above.

<u>The Old Rules vs. The New Rules</u>. The old rules of investing were pretty simple. Diversify your portfolio among a wide range of U.S. stocks, mutual funds and bonds; ride out the ups and downs; keep a long-term horizon and resist the urge to sell stocks during market declines. If you followed these rules, your portfolio would grow and you would be in great shape for the 4th quarter – or so Wall Street would have you believe.

As many of you have found out the hard way, these rules don't work quite as well as they used to. In fact, it is questionable whether they work at all given that many investors have actually lost money in the U.S. stock market over the past ten years. Instead, in order to successfully navigate the 4th quarter, I suggest you adhere to a new set of rules that take into account the shifting nature of the markets and world economy.

<u>Buy and Hold is a Strategy, Not a Commandment.</u> How many times have we been told that the only way to succeed as an investor is to hold stocks for the long-term? According to many on Wall Street, selling stocks is for suckers. Once you buy a stock or mutual fund you just need to hold on for the ride higher and any attempt to sell the thing before then is downright un-American.

I've got news for you, selling stocks is how you make money. Buying something with the idea of holding it until perpetuity is a tough business. It works for Warren Buffett, but for most of us mere mortals it requires an

17

The Transition

almost super-human amount of prescience.

Instead, let me suggest a different strategy. Buy stocks and mutual funds with the specific plan of selling them. In fact, go so far as to determine when you will sell them before you ever buy the first share.

For example, when you buy a stock know exactly how much of a loss you are willing to take on it. It could be a set dollar amount, a percentage of your original investment, or any other figure you like. The important thing is that you know how much downside you are willing to take before you enter the position.

Conversely, be willing to sell part of your holdings as the stock or fund goes higher. For example, if you are fortunate enough to have a stock that climbs higher by 30%, why not sell a quarter of it? You lock in a small profit, free up capital for other opportunities and provide yourself with leeway to hold the remainder of your position through market gyrations, content with the fact you've already taken some profits along the way.

The idea that everyone should be a buy-and-hold investor is simply wrong. Buying and holding a stock is a strategy, it is not a commandment. This strategy works in long-term bull markets like we saw in the 1980s and 1990s, but it does not work particularly well in other types of markets. Know the type of market you are working with and invest accordingly.

<u>Diversification Post 2008</u>. Diversification is a term that's thrown around a lot in investment circles. It is a simple concept best expressed by the old English proverb "don't put all your eggs in one basket." Or, as the legendary Greek philosopher Socrates more artfully put it, "everything in moderation."

So what does this have to do with investing during the

Financial Planning

4th quarter? Everything. The whole idea behind portfolio diversification is to reduce overall investment risk. And in the 4th quarter, managing risk is the key to investment success.

Unfortunately, most investors—individual and professional alike—misunderstand the concept of diversification. It does not mean owning a lot of different things in your portfolio. Instead, it means owning the right mix of things in your portfolio. In fact, constructing a diversified investment portfolio is a lot like putting together a puzzle—all the pieces need to fit together for it to work.

Let me give you an example. If I have a portfolio that includes five U.S. stocks, most people will agree it is poorly diversified. But what if I owned 100 U.S. stocks, would that provide better diversification? Surprisingly, it wouldn't.

Portfolio diversification has very little to do with the number of stocks you own. After all, whether you own five or 500 U.S. stocks, the vast majority of them are going to decline during a market sell-off. And, while having more stocks insulates you from company-specific bad news, it does nothing to protect you during broad market downturns.

Now take a look at a portfolio that has some U.S. stocks, some international stocks, some bonds, some real estate and some natural resources. During a broad decline in the U.S. stock market, your U.S. stock positions will almost certainly decline. But your bond positions will likely gain ground. Depending on the environment, your international stock, real estate and natural resources might also keep chugging along. And so your overall portfolio, while possibly not providing earth-shattering gains, likely won't fall off a cliff either.

As you may have already guessed, the secret to proper diversification is not the number of things you own, but

The Transition

rather the correlations between the things you own. Or, put another way, if you make sure to fill your investment portfolio with a handful of different investments, none of which go up and down in unison, you will have a much better chance of riding out a market downturn than if you own hundreds of securities, all of which are leveraged to the performance of one particular market.

So my advice to you as you enter the 4th quarter is to sit down with your current investment portfolio and take a good, hard look at exactly what you own. Filter through the labels like small-cap growth and large-cap value since history shows us that these distinctions mean very little in a major market downturn. Instead, focus on the correlations between the different types of investments you own. What you find may surprise you.

Getting Help. Properly managing your financial affairs during the 4th quarter of life is critical to being able to enjoy your hard-earned retirement. This has never been more true than in today's turbulent market. An obvious question is whether you should try to handle the task yourself or seek outside help.

Like a lot of things in life, there is no right answer. I know very successful retirees who manage their own investments and do exceptionally well. I know others who would never imagine trying to navigate the financial market's crosscurrents without professional help.

The only guidance I can give in this regard is the following; be honest with yourself. Managing investments is not rocket science and success is rarely dependant on one's intelligence. Or, put another way, almost everyone reading this book is smart enough to manage his own investments.

The difference between succeeding or failing is less

Financial Planning

about "smarts" and more about discipline and interest. It is about a willingness to devote time and effort to investing that could otherwise be devoted to other pursuits like travel, family or hobbies. If you enjoy pouring over stock and mutual fund research, analyzing economic issues, and can remain calm even during major market downturns, managing your own money may be a perfect fit. If you would rather be playing golf, you might want to find a professional to help you.

If you do decide to seek investment assistance, you will likely confront an issue common to almost all investors—how do I select someone to help me? After all, while there is no shortage of people who would love to help you invest your money, finding someone reputable, qualified, and primarily concerned with your welfare, not his own, can be a daunting task. Here are some questions you should consider asking during your search.

1. What are your qualifications?

The terms "investment advisor" and "financial planner" are used by many financial professionals. Ask the planner what qualifies him to offer financial-planning advice and whether he is recognized as a Certified Financial Planner (CFP), a Certified Public Account-Personal Financial Specialist (CPA-PFS), Charter Financial Analyst (CFA), or other similar designation.

2. What services do you offer?

The services a financial planner offers depend on a number of factors including credentials, licenses, and areas of expertise. Some planners offer financial-planning advice on a range of topics, but do not sell financial products.

The Transition

Others may provide advice only in specific areas, such as estate planning or tax matters. During the 4th quarter, you will likely need help in a variety of areas like investing, estate planning, insurance, cash flow planning, and tax advice—make sure you know with which of these areas a prospective advisor can help.

3. How are you compensated?

As part of your financial-planning agreement, the financial planner should clearly tell you in writing how he will be paid for the services to be provided. Planners can be paid in several ways:

- A salary paid by the company for which the planner works. The planner's employer receives payment from you or others, either in fees or commissions, in order to pay the planner's salary.

- Fees based on an hourly rate, a flat rate, or on a percentage of your assets and/or income.

- Commissions paid by a third party from the products sold to you to carry out the financial-planning recommendations. Commissions are usually a percentage of the amount you invest in a product.

- A combination of fees and commissions, whereby fees are charged for the amount of work done to develop financial-planning recommendations and commissions are received from any products sold. In addition, some planners may offset some portion of the fees you pay if they receive commissions for

Financial Planning

carrying out their recommendations.

4. How much do you typically charge?

While the amount you pay the planner will depend on your particular needs, the financial planner should be able to provide you with an estimate of possible costs based on the work to be performed.

Such costs should include the planner's hourly rates or flat fees, or the percentage he would receive as commission on products you may purchase as part of the financial-planning recommendations.

Also, make sure to check whether there are any other fees in addition to the management fee the advisor charges. For example, transaction fees, hourly data processing charges, wire fees and planning-related charges can add up to big dollars over the course of an advisory relationship.

5. Describe any conflicts of interest you may have in representing me.

Some business relationships with a planner could have conflicts that affect his professional judgment while working with you, inhibiting the planner from acting in your best interest.

Ask the planner to provide you with a description in writing of his conflicts of interest. For example, financial planners who sell insurance policies, securities or mutual funds have a business relationship with the companies that provide these financial products. The planner may also have relationships or partnerships that should be disclosed to you such as business he receives for referring you to an insurance agent, accountant or attorney for implementation of planning suggestions.

The Transition

6. Have you ever been disciplined for unlawful or unethical actions in your professional career?

Several government and professional organizations regulate various aspects of the financial services industry. Just to be safe, you should check with the Securities & Exchange Commission, your state insurance and securities departments and the Certified Financial Planning Board regardless of the answer you receive from the planner.

7. Can I have it in writing?

Ask the planner to provide you with a written agreement that details the services that will be provided. Keep this document in your files for future reference. If the planner refuses to provide you with a written agreement, I would suggest finding someone else.

Coping With The Emotional Side Of Investing

To paraphrase former New York Yankee catcher Yogi Berra, "Investing is 90% mental. The other half is physical." In fact, having invested both professionally and in my own account for over twenty years, I can tell you that the emotional side of investing is by far the most important to success.

Investing is an incredibly difficult endeavor. The stress of buying and selling securities is difficult in the best of circumstances and downright painful in challenging markets. Compound that with the fact that even the most successful investors are rarely right more than half the time and you can see why investing often wreaks havoc on the psyche of many individual investors.

Financial Planning

To succeed you have to be able to master your emotions. Buying when the markets are screaming higher and selling at market bottoms aren't rational decisions. None of us would take such action after thoughtful reflection. Yet these are exactly the actions historically undertaken by millions of individual investors since the Amsterdam Stock Exchange first opened its doors to public equities in 1602.

So how can you reign in your emotions enough to allow you a fair shot at succeeding as an investor? Although there is no easy answer, I can provide three pieces of advice that may help.

First, heed the old adage, "knowledge is power." Nowhere is that more true than in investing. If you know what you own and why you own it, you are much less likely to act precipitously even during a market panic. Acquiring this knowledge is not easy, but in my opinion it is impossible to invest without it.

Second, develop a plan and force yourself to stick to it. For example, if you have decided to sell any stock you own if it loses more than 10 percent of its value, then do not deviate from this plan. I can guarantee it will not be easy. You will want to keep holding the stock until it gets back to even, or you will believe it is still a great company and simply misunderstood by Wall Street. Ignore all these thoughts. If your plan says to sell the stock if it loses 10 percent then do it. The largest losses I have ever taken as an investor were because I failed to stick to my plan and held onto a stock because I was convinced I knew more about its true value than anyone else.

Finally, learn to forgive yourself. I cannot count all the mistakes I have made as an investor. I made them when I first started investing money and I still make them now. The difference is that I learned along the way to not dwell

The Transition

on them. If you make a mistake as an investor, act quickly to correct it and move on. It will not be your last one, believe me, but you will gain nothing by beating yourself up over a bad decision.

Taxes And Inflation – They Are Both Going Higher

Since early 2008, the Federal Reserve along with the U.S. Treasury Department have taken a variety of aggressive steps to stem the economic crisis. These have ranged from direct injections of capital into most of our nation's major financial institutions to historically-large purchases of Treasury instruments by the Federal Reserve to pump much needed liquidity into the system.

While the measures taken have been varied, the ultimate consequences of most of these measures are the same. The Federal government is going to have to print a lot of money – which will likely cause inflation to move significantly higher over the next several years – and it is going to have to raise taxes considerably to pay for all the spending it is undertaking. As a result, in order to prosper during the coming years, you need to know how to deal with higher taxes and higher inflation.

Taxes: The IRS Never Retires. Many people entering this transitional time presume that, when they retire, so does the Internal Revenue Service. After all, if you are no longer generating employment income, what exactly is the IRS going to tax?

And while that is true to a point, the ever-resourceful IRS still has a few tricks up its sleeve. For example, the IRS will gladly tax the income you receive from your investments, as well as the gains you generate when you sell a security or mutual fund.

Financial Planning

Not content to stop there, the IRS will also tax the money you take out of your retirement plans, whether they are traditional individual retirement accounts (IRA) or employer-run 401(k) plans. In fact, the IRS gets almost giddy at the prospect of taxing money coming out of one of your retirement accounts, since it can not only tax the gains you have made on your investments within the plans, it can generally tax every single dollar you pull out—whether gains or initial investment—and it can do so at your ordinary income tax rate, rather than the more advantageous capital gains tax rate.

Think about this for a second if you are relying on the savings in your IRA or 401(k) account to fund all or part of your retirement. Depending on your tax bracket and state of residence, you could end up paying a third (or more) of your hard-earned retirement savings to the government. That simple and often overlooked fact can put a huge crimp in your retirement if you don't plan ahead.

Just to compound those potential tax problems, as you enter the 4th quarter, you will almost certainly lose many of your most advantageous tax deductions. For example, your business-related tax deductions and pre-tax retirement plan contribution deductions generally fall by the wayside when you retire.

While coping with these tax issues is not necessarily easy, there are a few pieces of advice I can offer to help you tackle the problem.

<u>Make Sure to Offset Your Gains and Losses</u>. When you sell a profitable investment, you normally pay taxes on the gain. One way to reduce your taxes is to also sell some of your losing investments. You can then offset your gains and losses, wiping out all or a portion of your investment-related tax bill.

The Transition

For example, let's say you have a $1,000 gain on one stock, and a $1,000 loss on another. If you sell only your profitable stock, you will owe taxes on the $1,000 gain. But if you sell both stocks, your $1,000 gain will be offset by your $1,000 loss. That's good news from a tax standpoint, since it means you don't have to pay taxes on either position. Just watch out for the confusingly-named "wash sale rule," which precludes you from repurchasing the losing security within 30 days of selling it.

Keep Track of Your Mutual Fund Distributions. If your investment portfolio is anything like mine, it has a combination of individual stocks, mutual funds, bonds, and maybe even a few other types of investments. While keeping track of most of these for tax purposes is fairly straight-forward, there is a potentially expensive wrinkle that comes into play when dealing with mutual funds.

Calculating your gains and losses from the sale of an individual stock is fairly straight-forward. Your basis is simply the price you paid for the shares (including commissions), and the gain or loss is the difference between your basis and the net proceeds from the sale. However, it gets more complicated when dealing with mutual funds.

When calculating your basis in a mutual fund, it's easy to forget to include the dividends and capital gains distributions you reinvested in the fund. The IRS considers these distributions as taxable earnings in the year they're made. As a result, you have already paid taxes on them. By failing to add these distributions to your basis, you may end up reporting a larger gain than necessary when you ultimately sell the fund.

Put Your Investments in the Right Accounts. As a

Financial Planning

general rule, you should put investments that produce lots of taxable income or short-term capital gains in your tax-advantaged accounts, while investments that pay dividends or produce long-term capital gains should be held in your traditional accounts.

For example, let's say you own 500 shares of General Electric (GE) and intend to hold them for several years. This investment will generate quarterly dividend payments and a long-term capital gain or loss when sold, both of which will be taxed at 15% or less. Since these shares already have favorable tax treatment, you gain very little by sheltering them in a tax-advantaged account.

In contrast, most bonds produce a steady stream of interest income. Since this income doesn't qualify for special tax treatment, you will have to pay taxes on it at your marginal rate. Unless you are in a very low tax bracket, holding these investments in a tax-advantaged account makes sense because it allows you to defer these tax payments far into the future, or possibly avoid them altogether.

None of these tips will completely solve the unique investment tax issues facing many retirees on their own, but, in combination, they can make a difference. And if you are anything like most retirees, you will likely agree that every little bit counts.

<u>Inflation: Up, Up, And Away</u>. The second outgrowth of the Federal government's largess aimed at combating the economic crisis will almost certainly be higher inflation. As famed economist Milton Friedman once remarked, "inflation is always and everywhere a monetary phenomenon." Or put differently, when the Federal Reserve prints money it will generally cause higher inflation; when they print a lot of money, it will almost

The Transition

certainly do so. Given the extreme amounts of liquidity being pumped into the system recently, it is hard to imagine inflation is far behind.

For many people coming out of the recent economic crisis, they want nothing more than the safety and security of shifting what is left of their investments into bonds, particularly if they are near retirement.

And that may be entirely appropriate if you already have all the money you need to not only retire, but also to keep you in comfort for the next 20, 30 or even 40 years. For those of us without multi-million dollar investment portfolios, though, shifting all of our investments into low or no-growth investments may not be the best decision.

The Problem

When Germany's Kaiser Willhelm first set the age for mandatory retirement at 65 in the late 1800s, nobody paid much attention to retirement planning. After all, since the average life expectancy at the time was only 47 years, anyone who made it to "mandatory retirement age" in the 19th century was clearly living on borrowed time.

In contrast, it is now generally accepted among gerontologists that average life expectancies in the U.S. and other developed countries may soon exceed 85 years. And with the rapid advancement in the medical and biotechnology arenas, it is not hard to imagine we may someday see average lifespans in the triple digits.

While this is great news, it also brings with it some financial challenges. After all, if your investments need to last you another 10, 15, or even 20 years, they not only need to be safe, they need to grow. Otherwise, you will likely run out of money long before your time.

Financial Planning

This potential problem is even more pronounced when we look at the likely escalation in costs for items like food, energy and health care over the next few decades. For example, a recent study by Fidelity Investments found that a 65-year-old couple retiring today would need $215,000 set aside just to pay for medical expenses for the next 20 years. A similar analysis by the Employee Benefit Research Institute was even more sobering, estimating that the same 65-year-old couple would need, assuming average life expectancy of 82 for men and 85 for women, more than $300,000 set aside to pay for health-care costs in retirement, and more than $550,000 if the couple lives to age 92.

The (Partial) Solution

Let me take this full circle, back to the opening premise that people who have been burned during the current market decline may now be committed to casting aside their stock investments in favor of bonds and cash once they start heading towards retirement. That strategy—which has been taken as gospel for decades by investors—may not be as appropriate now as it was in the past.

Few people would argue that a 40-year-old investor should convert his investment portfolio into bonds to avoid taking undue risk. In fact, for most investors that age, having anything more than a small allocation to bonds would seem overly cautious. After all, they have 25 more years until retirement, and history has taught us that, over such a long period of time, the equity markets outperform bonds by leaps and bounds.

Now look at a 65-year-old investor who has just retired. Conventional wisdom would dictate that he adopt an extremely conservative portfolio. Some experts recommend

The Transition

as much as 70 to 80 percent of his portfolio should go into bonds, with only a token allocation to equities or other types of investments.

What these experts fail to grasp is that the 65-year-old investor may have another 20, 25 or even 30 years during which his portfolio must not only provide him with funds to cover all or a part of his expenses, but also keep pace with inflation to protect his purchasing power. This extended time frame—courtesy of our ever-increasing average life expectancies—means that ordinary bond investments with little growth and moderate yield simply won't cut it alone.

Instead, unless you already have all the money you will ever need for retirement, you should consider a portfolio strategy that not only reduces risk—since you are likely not in the position to recoup large portfolio losses—but also provides you with long-term portfolio growth. And while there are a variety of specific strategies they can consider, almost all of them will involve at least some exposure to stocks.

Discovering the Value(s) of Money

As you would expect, I have spent most of this chapter discussing how to manage your investments during the 4th quarter of life and some of the common pitfalls that often plague retirees.

Most of us learned the value of money when we were young. I just wish I had paid more attention to these lessons once I grew up. Earning an allowance for doing chores around the house, mowing the neighbor's lawn, and setting up lemonade stands on hot summer days all taught us concepts like entrepreneurship and the meaning of hard work.

Financial Planning

Unfortunately, unless you were very lucky, nobody ever taught you what to do with that money once you earned it, beyond perhaps setting up a simple savings account. In fact, concepts like investment management, basic accounting principles and taxation are completely foreign to most children and to many adults as well.

One of the greatest gifts you can give to both your children and grandchildren is an understanding of these concepts so that they can avoid many of the financial mistakes we have all made during our lifetimes. I'm not talking about giving your money to your children, funding their college or other education or financing their travel or business ventures. I am instead addressing the unique ability of people entering the 4th quarter to impart the financial knowledge they have gained over their lifetimes to help teach their children about wealth and the ways one can obtain, keep and use this wealth.

There are myriad ways someone entering the 4th quarter of life can pass along their financial knowledge. Helping their children open and maintain banking and brokerage accounts, offering to teach them about the values of home ownership, and working with them to understand the need to save and invest throughout their lives can all be invaluable.

Conclusion

I know from watching my parents, clients and friends enter the 4th quarter of life that it can be financially daunting. The rules of the game change substantially in the 4th quarter. Making money gives way to preserving it, and the margin for error declines dramatically.

But remember that if approached correctly, the 4th

The Transition

quarter can also be the most financially rewarding. In fact, at no point in your life will you ever have more control over your financial destiny. And, with the proper amount of planning and common sense, your hard-earned savings can provide you with the flexibility and freedom to truly enjoy the 4th quarter of your life.

Financial Planning

DAVID A. TWIBELL, J.D.
President – Wealth Management
Colorado Capital Bank
5251 DTC Parkway, Suite 1120
Greenwood Village, Colorado 80111
(303) 814-5545
dtwibell@coloradocapitalbank.com

David Twibell directs Colorado Capital Bank's wealth management practice. He provides portfolio management and wealth advisory services to individuals, trusts, charitable organizations and privately-owned businesses.

David writes about portfolio management and retirement planning for several national financial publications, including *Financial Planning, Financial Advisor,* and *Physician's Money Digest.* He is also frequently quoted by the national media, including *The Wall Street Journal, The Journal of Financial Planning, Money, CNN* and *CNBC,* on issues such as alternative investments, portfolio management and retirement planning.

He received his B.S. in Finance from Santa Clara University, magna cum laude, in 1988, and his J.D. from University of California at Berkeley, Order of the Coif, in 1991.

Chapter Two
Why the "Point of Transition" is so Important

As a young business man, I took great pleasure and pride in mentoring young people who were either still in high school and college, or starting their business careers. On reaching age 60, my plan was to wind down my business and devote time again to mentoring those who could benefit from my knowledge and experience. But at the same time I began planning how I would share this information, I discovered that today's younger generation no longer listened to me as their predecessors had. I was surprised and concerned. The message was still the same and even stronger than before. What had changed? I finally got my answer.

While conducting research for a new senior community I was developing, I was also attending

The Transition

seminars on the different traits between groups known as the Greatest Generation, the Baby Boomers, Generation X and the Millennium, or Generation Y, group. But, even with my new education about Generations X and Y, I still didn't understand why my mentoring contributions were being brushed aside by them. The answer came in an encounter at the Phoenix airport. I approached the security officer with my usual youthful step and air of confidence, handing her my ticket and identification. She looked at my license, then back to me, again at the license, again at me, and she asked me, in a stern but dry tone, "Did you dye your hair before?" I was appalled until I looked at the license and realized that, two years before when the picture was taken, my hair and mustache were dark brown. Now both are gray – with brown highlights! I hadn't noticed the change that occurred gradually over that time. But, though taken by surprise by her question, I took pride in my quick recovery when I replied, "No, I wasn't dying it then, but I am dying it gray now!"

As I sat that evening in the darkening terminal waiting for my flight, I could not shake the thought of what had just happened. I was a little hurt and quite shaken by her comments. I hadn't realized the image I was portraying to others, which was in direct contrast to how I viewed myself. Yes, I knew I was over 60 years old and what that meant, but I hadn't understood what that meant to others. I made up my mind to turn it into a positive lesson, as opposed to viewing it as an attack on my image. "Of course!" I reasoned. "Now I understand why the younger people I was trying to mentor were not paying attention to me." My gray hair was immediately sending the message, "This guy is even older than my parents! They don't understand me so how could he understand me?"

With that dilemma resolved, I turned my attentions to

Why the "Point of Transition" is so Important

determining the direction I would take in using my time in the 4th quarter of my life. I thought about the passion I had always felt for helping others, and I knew this was the way I wanted to use this time. I had been successful in my business career, but I felt I had neglected my responsibility to give back. I stood and went to the window to watch a beautiful sunset. I thought about all of the wonderful senior communities that had been developed in the Phoenix area by Del Webb and the developers who followed. Returning to my seat, I began reading a magazine article about America being on the verge of an unprecedented social and marketing phenomenon. The article profiled the Baby Boomers, the generation born between 1946 and 1964. It is a force 76 million strong with an estimated spending power of two trillion dollars a year and in line to inherit seven trillion dollars from their parents. The Baby Boomers will define what it means to be a senior in America – not only through wealth and sheer numbers, but also because of the influence of this group that transformed our country in the 1960s. "Wow!" I thought. "This is **my** generation: this is me!" I knew immediately that this is the age group that I can mentor and assist through knowledge, experience and a heart-felt desire to help those who may be struggling at this time in their lives.

The next year was spent gathering thoughts, materials and resources, complied over the last 25 years during my business career, and I started writing this book. At 61, I began feeling the natural changes of this time of life. Some of these changes felt positive and some definitely negative. The welcome, positive feelings were easy to accept. I felt wiser about life than ever before. As I reflected on my grown children, I felt pride in who they had become. One of the wonderful changes was becoming a "grandpa" of four. There isn't anything that delights me more than hearing my

The Transition

grandchildren call out "Grandpa!" But, along with those positive changes, I was also experiencing changes decidedly negative. I had less energy and my graying hair reflected a different image to those around me than I still had of myself. Unless one shaves or applies makeup in very low lighting, or takes a shower blindfolded, it is difficult to ignore the new body changes and wrinkles that seem to appear on a daily basis. Yes, these changes are natural but hard to accept as a part of your identity, but I did discover that these negative feelings could be overcome by making adjustments in my lifestyle.

In coping with these changes, my hope is that reading this book will be as valuable to you as writing it has been for me. The difficulties I have encountered in transitioning to the 4th quarter of my life were the inspiration for writing the book. Helping others and giving back were the goals. The good news in the messages contained in this book have helped me immensely. Like many of you, it is difficult for me to listen to speakers who say they have the answers but have not experienced the life struggles that we have endured. It is similar to newlyweds who think they have all the answers to a successful marriage, or couples expecting their first baby who assure us their lifestyle will not change, as we admit ours did, when the child arrives. They all believe they have the answers and will handle it better by not making the mistakes we made. It is later on that nearly everyone realizes that they were wrong.

Transition is a challenge at any age. The specific purpose of the book is to assist the Baby Boomers in making a smooth transition into the 4th quarter of their lives by educating themselves about strong relationships, excellent health and financial well-being.

Now to the book's title: *The Transition – Winning the 4th Quarter of Life*. How was this title chosen? On reflection, I

Why the "Point of Transition" is so Important

saw that so much of the success in one's life is tied to how one transitions from one life experience, one time of life to the next: from high school to college, from single to married, from a house full of kids to an "empty nest", from the height of a career to retirement. This book is about that *point* of transition. What you do at that point of transition is key to the success of your retirement years. The smoother the transition is, the greater your success will be. In my business career, success has always been about making the right choices and knowing when to "pull the trigger." This book was written to assist you as you begin the 4th quarter of your life. Your successful transition will depend on the changes you make to maintain purpose and happiness in your life.

This book will define the tools you will need to make changes, to overcome adversity, to make good choices and develop a strong positive mental attitude. I believe that implementation of these tools is the pathway to success. Most of us think about the future and plan to do something about it, but many lack the direction to follow through on these plans because that is where all the hard work lies. Change is difficult. There is an old German proverb that states "To change and to change for the better are two different things."

Each chapter in this book is meant to be a tool to help implement these changes for the better that are necessary to the transition into the 4th quarter. In the following chapters, there is solid useful information about making good choices and overcoming adversity. I will describe how the right attitude is 90% of the battle in dealing with any problem. You will also see how these tools, as well as examples of life experiences, will show how perseverance can overcome most any adversity. My favorite chapter is "Organization and Goals." People going through transition who have written goals have a roadmap for the future.

The Transition

"Boomers" with knowledge on how to properly organize their lives can use these tools to compete with younger people who think more quickly and/or are more adept in the new cyber world. It is my favorite chapter because I get so much satisfaction out of being organized. It is enormously gratifying to see the results that occur after you have succeeded in what you set out to do – short-term accomplishments like finishing a task on your to-do list, or long-term goals like writing a book. These accomplishments will leave you with peace of mind and a tranquil spirit.

As you will discover, health and wealth are only two of the three key topics facing the Baby Boomers. In my view, the third topic is *the key to life*. It is about giving to and doing for others. In the 4th quarter, we now have the time to help. It could be that extra time you never had before to help your children and grandchildren, or that desire you have always had to serve those in your community who are less fortunate. By giving, you actually receive by improving your quality of life. This makes the 4th quarter of your life exciting and rewarding. After reading this book, I hope you will realize that your **reputation** is what you did for yourself. Your *legacy* is what you did for others.

Chapter Three
To Transition is to Change

In football, whether you are down by seven points or up by fourteen entering the 4th quarter, you don't win the game by playing just three quarters. The same is true of life. You must play the 4th quarter to win the game. America hasn't always allowed its seniors to play the 4th quarter. Often they were benched. You can't win the game of life from the bench. America's answer has been to say that it is a senior's obligation to leave the game. The Baby Boomer generation can't and won't accept that premise anymore. Through our sheer numbers, financial power and political clout, teamed with a strong commitment to change, the Boomers will insist on staying in the game and will actively enjoy this period in our lives. Throughout each quarter, Boomers have continued to

The Transition

break with tradition and are altering stereo-typical perceptions regarding age. Chronologically the Boomers may be aging, but in our thoughts and behaviors, we are anything but old! What the Baby Boomers have discovered, that is more important to us than any preceding generation, is that life is all about how you finish the game, not what the score was at halftime.

Transitioning into the 4th quarter is more unique than any other time in your life because, for the first time, there is more life behind you than in front of you. This hasn't been the case before. This means that you now must accept certain realities of life. In the first three quarters, you could hope for future change – the hope that things would change for the better, given time. How many times have we heard someone say, "If only I had known that when I was younger," or "If I could go back to school, I would pay attention this time!" This point in time is more about reality than hopes and dreams. The most difficult fact you always knew but now hits the hardest is that you can't "re-do" the past. Second chances were more readily available when we were young. But, as we advance in age and progress through life, those second chances keep dwindling until we arrive at the understanding that life is linear, and no one gets a second chance to do it all again.

The good news is that the most important part of life is still in front of those of us in transition, but whether the game will be won or lost will depend on how a person plays this 4th quarter. We can still win the "big game." I chose the word big instead of entire for a specific reason. Using "entire" suggests that, to be a winner, you would have to be ahead in the game up to now. That is not true. Success, being the winner, depends on how you finish the game. You must finish to win, and if you finish well, you are a success. No matter how the first quarters were played, you can still win

To Transition is to Change

the big game. Before the Boomer generation, sitting out the last quarter caused seniors to lose meaningful participation with a lot of living still ahead of them. They were told to rest on their laurels and not to worry about being out of the game. What a disappointment it has been for those who felt they hadn't previously been winners and who were now denied the opportunity to change the outcome of the game of their life. It was also disappointing for those entering the 4th quarter as a success, to have to declare themselves winners knowing that they had 25% of their lives still in front of them. Once we acknowledge that we must continually transition in life, the most difficult task to perform for people of all ages, is to make those changes.

Whether change happens naturally or is carefully planned, most people are resistant to it. As a result, change becomes a major roadblock to altering your life. In most cases, resistance to change comes from fear of the unknown. We should no longer have this fear when approaching the 4th quarter because we know that life itself is change. Since change is inevitable, why not view it as a positive force rather than a negative experience. This time in your life is all important. You will be experiencing changes both mentally and physically which will change your daily routine. The bottom line is that these changes and this transition affect your "identity." The better you plan for the transition, the happier your life will be.

What has helped me deal with changes is to approach them gradually. We know that drastic change, whether in habits or lifestyle, always produces stress. This stress is typically negative, affecting change and growth. When making changes gradually, a better understanding develops and feelings are much more positive. Abrupt change does not allow us to have a true understanding of what is happening to us. Gradual change lets us approach the future

The Transition

with a sense of direction and purpose, allowing us to inch into uncharted waters without jumping in with both feet. Change becomes a positive, conscious choice, instead of something forced on us. Aging is not a choice, but *how* we age is.

As you will see in the ensuing chapters, I have always been an enthusiastic proponent of the power of "Organization and Goals." Before I write my goals down, I outline a page called PREMISES that identifies where I am at that particular point in time so that my aspirations are applicable and ultimately attainable. Throughout my life, I have discovered that most of my sense of self came through my business career and civic accomplishments. Now, with this identity behind me, the very thought of using the words "semi-retired" or "retired" was not only foreign to me but also frightening. I needed to proceed, no matter what, and make the changes necessary to my life. I did two things that helped me make the transition. First, I coined the term "flexing down." This is the term I chose to use instead of "slowing down" or being "semi-retired." This term meant to me a slower change and a gradual recognition of my age with a nod to the energy I still felt, and with a need to implement a new plan. Flexing down sounds action-oriented, making this period of change a positive experience. I was making the changes work *for* me. My fear had been that these changes would result in the loss of everything I had grown accustomed to using to define myself. But, instead, I felt encouraged about all of the new experiences ahead of me as I followed my written goals for the coming year, embracing the "flexing down" concept.

How is the concept of "flexing down" defined? While attending a patients' safety conference as a hospital board director, I heard a staff member say to the chief nursing officer, "I am going to take some flex time next week." I

To Transition is to Change

had been drafting my yearly goals, using the term semi-retirement. But this term, flex, immediately caught and held my attention. I was unfamiliar with the term so I asked the nursing officer what the staff member meant by flex time. Flex time, she explained, differs from vacation time in that your vacation is scheduled in advance but flex time is used when you feel the need for some extra physical or emotional rest. With this in mind, I returned to writing my yearly goals, deleting the phrase semi-retirement and adding this: "Since I am feeling the need to make changes, I will make those changes gradually and spend this year 'flexing down' in my professional life." By writing this down, I felt I now had a vehicle in place for dealing with those emotional and physical changes ahead of me.

Even though my year of flexing down was very successful, I did notice emotional and physical changes in my life and daily routine. As a result, I labeled the next year's goals as "adjusting to change." Change is inevitable, but only the successful ones adjust to those changes. Now, as the new year approached, I needed to finish my three-year adjustment plan in order to move smoothly into my own 4th quarter. This would be my year of transition in that I finally had the extra time for those who are most important in my life, as well as the time to take on new challenges.

The following is an example of the master plan premise for gradual change over a three-year period.

The Transition

MASTER PLAN

YEAR ONE PREMISES (Flexing Down)

1. The work I know and love is no longer challenging. I need new stimulus.

2. It is important to know when the party is over and when it is time to move on to the next event.

3. It is natural that I should feel the need for change and I should not be concerned that I feel this way. Usually when one begins to feel this way, they tend to ignore the voice telling them to stop and listen.

By planning well and adjusting gradually, anyone can avoid the intimidating moment that signals the end of one's career.

YEAR TWO PREMISES (Adjusting to Change)

1. Re-evaluate personal objectives, taking into consideration age, cash flow, net worth and changing personal interests.

2. Make decisions and act without delay since what used to be is no longer applicable.

3. Relax, and change routine in order to create freshness, flexibility and open-mindedness.

To Transition is to Change

YEAR THREE PREMISES
(Extra Time/New Challenges)

1. Step back and view who you are and where you have been in order to determine where you want to go. Take the time to achieve neglected personal goals.

2. Make lifestyle decisions that reflect the world in which you are comfortable. You will know you have made the wrong choices if your life no longer resembles you.

3. Stay balanced. Stay active and involved but take time to relax and escape.

4. Establish healthy activities in order to maintain good health. Make it your goal to be in the best physical shape since your youth.

5. Thought – most of us don't mind getting older, just so long as we can function in the life to which we have grown accustomed and can do all the things we are used to doing. Being older is not the problem. Not being able to do the things you want and need to do is the issue.

I began feeling excited about my new-found freedom: the freedom of having extra time and opportunity for challenges. But the most exciting moment is when the transition takes place, and a whole new game begins in this quarter of life. The key word is "new."

The 4th quarter is the crucial quarter in the game. The original playbook is replaced with a new playbook, and the

The Transition

offensive and defensive tactics in life play out differently than in the first three quarters. Having this new playbook liberated me because it kept me in the game. I realized I was valuable and could be an important player on any team at this stage in my life. I could easily make the shift from speed and endurance, to the position of using the power of experience and influence. I no longer required the speed and agility of youth. With my *experience*, I was the one who could win the game. Instead of leaving the game, we Boomers can shift from the old playbook to the new.

One of the most important elements for achieving a successful transition is allowing that shift in your thinking. It is this shift that allows the transition to occur. Without actually changing the way you think, life may seem okay for awhile, but when the positive mind set is resisted, problems will develop mentally, emotionally and physically.

Chapter Four
When Adversity Hits and Choices are Made

Have you ever wondered why some people can overcome their problems with seeming ease and others can't? Have you ever reflected on your past and remembered how one or two adverse events changed everything and stopped you from having the life of your dreams?

Adversity can happen at any point in life. Who would have ever guessed we would be facing a national financial upheaval of this magnitude at this point in our lives. Just as the proper tools are required to fix your car, you need the proper tools and knowledge of how to use them in order to beat the adversity in your life and progress to the happy and fulfilling life you have in mind.

As we transition into the 4th quarter of our lives,

The Transition

knowing how to overcome adversity is more crucial than at any time before. Not only will the challenges become harder and the choices more difficult to make, but there may be more people in your life depending on your wisdom and experience. Often, earlier in your life, adversity could be swept under the rug and ignored, with the consequences not too severe. This is not the case now. If an adverse event like the Financial Crisis of 2008 occurs, it must be dealt with swiftly and correctly before more problems develop. Entering the 4th quarter, we are often the patriarch or matriarch of our families, becoming an important consultant to family members. Our advice will be needed to help others in everything from dealing with the death of parents to the troubles our children and grandchildren will face in their own lives.

The transition into the 4th quarter of life truly began for me with the sudden deaths of both my parents within an eight-day period. This happened just months before my 60th birthday. Losing them so close together made me feel like an orphan, even at 60. As the oldest sibling, I knew that I had become the patriarch and that I needed to accept that responsibility for the comfort of all the loved ones who would now depend on my life experiences and wisdom, as they once had depended on our parents. There is nothing more traumatic in life than the death of a loved one. Love is one of the strongest emotions we feel and the death of a loved one has a finality that forces us to examine our own lives, to be strong for those left behind.

Because of a bizarre sequence of events, my parents were admitted to the hospital on the same evening. My father had been in severe pain from what would later be diagnosed as colon cancer. He accidentally fell, knocking down my mother who was checking on him before going to bed. She fell to the floor, fracturing her pelvis and wrist.

When Adversity Hits and Choices are Made

My father died in the hospital following colon surgery and my mother was subsequently transferred to a nursing home. She was not recovering well. I promised her during an afternoon visit that I would stop by the next morning before meeting with the minister and the funeral home to arrange my father's funeral. As I sat with her that next morning, her breathing did not sound good and I told her that I would return right after the meetings were over. When I returned to the nursing home, the doctor met me at the door and advised me that my mother had only hours to live. My brother and I were at her side when she passed away that night. Early the following morning, I had to return to the funeral home to change the arrangements to a double service. Knowing that I was an organized person, the funeral director and minister smiled as I entered, saying "Okay, what did we forget to do?" I had to inform them that my mother had passed away the previous night and that I was now there to make the arrangements to combine my parents' funerals. As I contemplated this terrible adversity, I can honestly say that I can't remember ever having a tougher day.

Knowing the steps required in overcoming adversity helped me through that awful time and guided me in the months that followed. I needed to accept the finality – that they were both gone and would never return. I needed to create a plan to deal with what happened to them medically, to settle their estate, to deal with their personal property and belongings, and all that entailed. I needed to believe that I had done the right things before and after their deaths. And finally, I needed to make a choice – a hard choice – to be strong for my children and move forward, while honoring the memory of my parents.

Overcoming adversity requires following these steps, *in order*. Each is individually important. The steps are as

The Transition

follows: 1) Accept the adversity; 2) Create a comprehensive plan; 3) Re-establish pride and confidence; and 4) Make a choice.

Step 1 is first because it is so critical: accept the adversity that has challenged you. If the problem is not of your making, refuse to wallow in self-pity, bemoaning what has happened to you. Acceptance may be as simple as recognizing *no one* escapes sorrow and misfortune. If you caused or contributed to the adversity, admitting fault and taking responsibility for what has happened will allow you to progress to the next steps. If you are responsible for the problem and choose to place the blame elsewhere, you can't continue in a positive way. Not being honest with yourself hinders you from Steps 2 and 3: creating a plan and establishing pride and confidence. Honesty, combined with humility, is a crucial element in moving forward.

The second step is to create a comprehensive plan that includes a *written* timeline. Wouldn't it be wonderful if planning was actually taught in school or by your family? But good planning is more often self taught – if you're lucky.

As you will see in the chapter on organization, nothing is more powerful than a well thought-out plan. In constructing this plan, the main pitfall to avoid is the quick answer or overnight solution. No matter how appealing a short cut may seem, it is never the real and lasting solution. It will take a well-conceived plan, with the flexibility to allow for fine tuning and adjustments. The plan is all-important because it will keep you on course. You won't be side-tracked by others or by self-doubt. With a well-conceived and written plan, you will have a tangible way to analyze events when something does go wrong. The plan will provide a roadmap for your accomplishments, one that you can revise as needed, to keep you moving forward. The

When Adversity Hits and Choices are Made

plan also helps identify what works, what doesn't and what you must change. Without a written plan, most people become frustrated and overwhelmed, and abandon the challenges of overcoming adversity. It is essential to the plan that care be taken in writing it. Since I believe that problem-solving is the key to a happy life, Chapter Seven is my favorite. This is the chapter that Baby Boomers will need to stay in the game and play the 4th quarter of their lives.

The third step, often ignored, is the re-establishment of pride and confidence. When self worth is attacked, one can become negative and depressed. You may recall watching a sporting event during which an outstanding player – or entire team's – confidence is destroyed by adverse events. Without confidence, every play seems to end badly. Confidence is what allows you to play at the level necessary to win in overcoming adversity.

It is finally time to take Step 4. It may not be the most important but it can't be avoided. This step is about making hard choices, the first of which is usually either accepting the adversity or not. If we don't, we often end up indulging in self pity. People usually can't accept adversity if they haven't learned the tools to overcome it.

Adversity comes in two forms – those over which we have control and those over which we have no control. Both are equally difficult to accept. Why? Because, in either case, you must release self-blame to proceed. You must learn to laugh or cry at what has occurred and *move on*. When you can do this, you will be able to show compassion for others in their suffering.

One of the noticeable characteristics of strong, successful people is pride, the good kind of pride that creates a positive mental attitude. Step 3, developing pride in yourself, is an element necessary for handling adversity.

The Transition

Pride gives you the strength you need to face each day and overcome the problem before it overpowers you. Pride shapes your life and assists by not allowing you to quit, or run and try to hide from your problems. Reflecting back on heroes in history, real or fictional, it was a good sense of pride that prevented their total defeat. That kind of pride will serve you well as you face adversity.

Once you have taken these steps, you may ask yourself, "What should I do now?" At this point, a choice must be made regarding how to resolve a specific problem. I see four categories of choice: good, bad, hard, easy. Making the good choice or the hard choice is obviously the most difficult. Bad choices, easy choices usually tend to further adversity as time goes on. I have identified two tools to aid you in making good choices, and making hard choices as well. Even when dealing with the most complex of adverse situations, the first technique – keep it simple – will work for you. Reduce everything to its simplest form. Any person, even under stress, can better resolve problems using the KISS theory (Keep It Simple, Stupid.) Breaking the problem down to its most basic form makes it easier to focus on the most important issues.

I keep a list of inspirational quotes and affirmations near at all times. They provide me with needed clarity. A favorite quote from Will Rogers states "If you find yourself in a hole, stop digging!" Isn't it strange that, in the face of most adversity, we continue to dig that hole?! In business negotiations, I always think of the line from a Kenny Rogers song, *The Gambler*: "You've got to know when to hold'em, know when to fold 'em, know when to walk away, and know when to run." Stay with the simple answers.

If only more could be done to help young adults understand that they need to play the hand they are dealt. It often comes down to applying the basic premises in the

When Adversity Hits and Choices are Made

song, whether it be in your marriage, with your health or in your career: the choice of when to hold 'em, fold 'em or walk away.

The second tool in making good choices is one I learned years ago as a young businessman. It is about making tough decisions by using the format of ideal solutions. These are the questions you ask yourself when trying to make a hard decision. Examples are "If I had total control of the situation, what would I do?" or "In a perfect world, I would…" Answering these hypothetical questions provides clarity. This tool, and keeping it simple, have shaped my life and have made all the difference in my overcoming adversity.

Let me share an example with you of another adversity in my life. Although not life threatening, it was life shaping, tearing my world apart and causing devastation and extreme emotional distress. When I started my business career, I had very little going for me. Upon getting out of the army after serving overseas, I had no idea how to get a job – a serious situation considering that I was married and had a small son. What transpired has allowed me to live "The American Dream."

I decided to take advantage of the GI bill to return to graduate school and adjust to my new life. Although I had the GI Bill, I still needed unemployment checks and food stamps to survive. After a short time of this lifestyle, I decided to get on with my life. With a U-Haul truck and $500 in my pocket, I packed my family and headed west to Colorado. After many trials and tribulations, I eventually thrived and enjoyed great success in real estate. Within twenty years, I had become a multi-millionaire. Then, in the late 1980s, my world collapsed when the Tax Reform Act of 1986 and the Savings and Loan crisis in 1987 destroyed the commercial real estate industry. I was

The Transition

literally back to having just $500 in my pocket.

During those first twenty years, I had a ritual. Every year in early January, at around 4:30 in the morning, I would sit in my office and write my annual goals, objectives and strategies. The office was obviously tranquil at that early hour. Armed with a cup of hot coffee, I did my most productive thinking. That year, after all that had happened, I felt very low, exhausted from battling my financial difficulties. In order to survive and settle outstanding loans, I had to sell everything I owned: my home, cars, ranch and all of my horses – everything I had earned throughout my years of success. I had just finished plowing several commercial parking lots during the night with a pickup that was my last remaining vehicle. I needed the cash. That early morning in the quiet darkness of my office, I began the task at hand – that of writing my goals for the current year as I had always done.

When no goals came to mind, I put my pen down and closed my eyes, wondering what I would do from this point forward. I had nearly resigned myself to being content with telling any future grandchildren that Grandpa had once been a very successful man, when it suddenly struck me: I still have choices! I could choose to live in the past or I could choose to get excited about tomorrow and the possibility of new victories down the road that lay ahead. Immediately, I made a promise to myself that I would be successful again and, instead of taking twenty years to do it, this time I would do it in ten. I was determined to double my previous worth in that shortened amount of time. The choice was made and I am happy to report that I was successful again, and that I more than doubled my net worth within ten years' time!

Many people have asked me how I managed to stay motivated on a daily basis during that four-year period of

When Adversity Hits and Choices are Made

financial devastation. In those years, I was constantly negotiating (fighting) with banks, living on a shoestring, selling assets and waging a two-year legal battle in federal court. In later chapters, I will cover every step, technique and tool I used to turn my fortunes around. **At the end of this book, I have included my personal journal describing my four years of adversity. I highly recommend you take a moment to read it as it may provide you with extra insight and assist you in persevering through your adversity!** I truly hope the information in these pages will provide a guideline for success to each and every reader. As you read later chapters, you will discover the answer is not only self-motivation, but also the motivation you will get from others. Motivation from others can be as obvious as being helped by teachers or other trained professionals, or it can be as unexpected as a late-night encounter with a very wise American Indian. The latter event is detailed in Chapter Six and was a turning point in my life. All experiences, large and small, can add up to help you through adversity.

In summary, the ideal solution is a very useful tool. It allows you to focus on the solution, not the problem. Ask yourself this: if I had total control over the solution to this problem, what would I do? Use that as a starting point. Attitudes are chosen. It is up to you. It *is* your choice whether your attitude is a positive or a negative one. Knowing that behavior determines results is key in looking for solutions. Isn't it exciting to realize that you can change your life by changing your attitude, to know that you are capable of improving your life by adopting a positive mindset? Again, changing your attitude may not be easy, and it doesn't happen overnight, but the rewards are worth the work and the wait. You need to clearly identify what your new attitude will be, and gather the affirmations that will help you change your old way of thinking.

Chapter Five
Everything is a Function of Attitude

Having a positive mental attitude must be very important. Libraries and bookstores have more shelves dedicated to that subject than any other. Books on this topic appear in all sections: religious, psychology and self-help. Is a positive attitude really that important in comparison to a person's appearance, education or financial status? You bet it is. Your attitude can most definitely alter your health and happiness.

A positive upbeat attitude is mandatory for a smooth transition. This may worry you if you are not feeling positive now, or if you have never had a positive attitude. The transition process is a great opportunity for you to change that. It is your choice. Maintaining a positive attitude is important for the entire 4th quarter of your life.

The Transition

Close your eyes and think of all the older people you have known since childhood. Despite their differences in gender, background and income, they can probably be divided into two basic categories: those who were happy and positive, and those who were not. Reflecting back, you can remember which were healthy and which weren't; those you wanted to spend time with and those you did not; those you enjoyed talking to and those you did not. It was all about attitude.

We know that we can't often control the negative forces that inevitably impact our lives. But we do have control in choosing the attitude we will embrace each day. As author Charles Swindol said, "I am convinced that life is 10% what happens to me and 90% how I react to it and so it is with you . . . we are in charge of our attitudes." We are never free from the inevitabilities of life – illness, accidents, natural disasters, but we are free to choose how we will respond to them.

Being an optimist at heart, I have always been annoyed by people who exhibit negative attitudes. I never understood why they could not change and view things in a more positive light. I was lucky enough to discover the answer to this question purely by chance one day after having the privilege of hearing a nationally known speaker. He had excited his audience with the power of positive thinking and its impact on future business endeavors. I left believing that *everyone* who attended must feel excited about life and just how good it can be. As I walked to the parking lot, I met a woman coming from the same lecture who looked as if she had just attended a funeral. Still excited and energized, I exclaimed, "Wasn't that an outstanding presentation?!" She replied, "You people will just never understand, will you?" This caught me off guard. "I'm not sure what you mean by you people," I countered.

Everything is a Function of Attitude

"I have attended these seminars for years and nothing ever changes." she explained. "I see the people go into the auditorium and I see them come out. It appears to me that those who go in with a positive mental attitude come out with a positive mental attitude, and those who go in feeling negative come out the same way. We negative people hear, listen, visualize and want to be positive but we don't understand how to change."

"So, what you are saying," I asked her, "is that you feel all the excitement and energy but you have no clue nor are you given any idea as to how to implement the changes necessary to maintain this attitude after you leave the seminar?"

"You are correct," she responded. "It is like being given something to assemble that has a color picture on the box, but no step-by-step instructions are provided." This explanation provided me with a great insight into why some people are always negative, and inspired me in my motivation to help others.

My feelings of dismay and annoyance with negative people made me very disappointed in myself. How had I missed the fact that, in most cases, negative people did not choose this mental attitude - that it might be genetics, or events that had happened during their lives? Whatever the cause, these people have never known how good a positive mental attitude feels or even what it is. I don't presume to provide an explanation for why this happens, but my hope is that they will be able to implement the concepts in this book to improve their lives by gaining that positive attitude that has eluded them. The key word is implementation.

Everything in life is a function attitude. A case in point is my daughter's father-in-law, Art Fisher. Art is 64 and the CEO of one of the largest lighting companies in Denver. In 1992, he had a medical checkup and was placed on a

The Transition

treadmill. During this test, the doctors noted a problem and stopped the test. A subsequent angiogram showed arterial blockage and he was advised to have immediate bypass surgery to repair five clogged arteries.

Just before the surgery, Art's doctor advised him that he did not have to have the surgery if he chose not to. Art was confused. He questioned the doctor. "I thought you and the other doctor said I had to do this. Are you now just trying to cover in case something goes wrong?" he asked. What else can I do, Art asked himself. He was already in the hospital so he decided he might as well have the surgery and get it over with. In retrospect, he wishes he had left the hospital that day and explored other options. Why? Because he is now legally blind as a result of the surgery. The operation lasted much longer than expected, a full 15 hours. Irregularities with the heart/lung machine and problems in the regulation of his blood pressure resulted in a condition that caused his blindness.

Despite this adversity, Art continues to be a successful businessman who appreciates the humor in every situation. His attitude is always positive, finding more good than bad in everything. With this adversity in his life that occurred through no fault of his own, I asked him how he has continued to persevere over the last 17 years. I asked him what his reaction was when he returned home for the first time, having to adjust to a new lifestyle. His first reaction was "Oh, crap!" and his second was concern for his wife. This would be a huge lifestyle adjustment for both of them. He proactively contacted doctors all around the United States in the hope of finding a way to correct his blindness. Finally, a top doctor in Berkley advised him that nothing could be done. His eyesight would not return. As that reality set in, for the first time he truly accepted what had happened to him. "Now what the hell are you going to do?"

Everything is a Function of Attitude

he asked himself. He decided to do everything he did before – with a few changes. He began socializing again, spending time with his children and, most importantly, he walked back through the main door of his office building without the use of a cane, and he got back to work. With a family to support and a company to run, Art decided to get on with it. And he did. Over the last 17 years, he has tripled the annual gross income of his company, despite his handicap!

Attitude is not as simple as just positive and negative. It is about identifying the positive to evaluate a situation, ranking the magnitude of the situation and making a plan for the solution. Art expressed dismay that people belabor things that happen to them, feeling that they can't do anything about them. He remembered the words of his high school football coach, "If you get knocked down, get back up so you can bleed again!" A simple understanding of the positives in his life made him aware of just how lucky he really was. He told me, "Even though I understood that I couldn't see, I knew I could still walk, talk, hear and use my brain to think. So everything has worked out okay." Art feels, more than anything, that adding humor to one's life greatly impacts their attitude. Because of that, he would like me to rename this chapter, "Everything is a Function of Humor."

My final question to Art – knowing how long he has been dealing with this – was "Are there times that you get angry or depressed about losing your sight?" His simple response was no. The reason for this is hope. He still maintains hope that one day a way to correct his blindness will be discovered. Art says, "Hope is a very big word. It is not a promise, but a feeling you get. I firmly believe I will see again before I die. It may be through surgery, the advancement of stem cell research, or it could just be a miracle!"

Chapter Six
Perseverance

*"It's not about getting knocked down;
it's about getting back up!"*
Rocky Balboa

Everyone will face some adversity in their lifetime. Some will be small problems that pass in the blink of an eye; some problems may last an entire lifetime. In order to overcome adversity, certain qualities and traits are necessary. You have heard it said that a person has a lot of "gumption", tenacity, strong will and other similar descriptions. These words describe perseverance, which is the essential trait required to overcome adversity. The word perseverance differs from other seemingly similar phrases such as "kick the habit', "get over it", "come around" or "beat it", in that when we think of perseverance, we think

The Transition

of the long term. We think of an issue that can't be solved quickly, an issue that causes us to dig deeper and work harder. Perseverance is one of the most powerful words in the English language and it is one of the most successful tools known to man. To persevere, you need to have self-discipline, remain focused on your main objective and be patient until things finally work for you. To persevere means you are in continual action, handling disappointment, frustration and even rejection. Those who persevere know that they cannot afford to let up. They know that victory is still within their grasp even though the scoreboard says they are behind.

Speaking of the scoreboard, please indulge my sharing a perfect example of belief and perseverance. The Fiesta Bowl football game between Boise State and Oklahoma on January 1, 2007, was a late night game and I remember falling asleep on the couch in front of the television while Boise State was being outmatched by Oklahoma. I woke up in time to witness one of the most dramatic finishes in college football history, a game that will keep people talking for years to come. Oklahoma and Boise State had scored a combined 22 points in the final 86 seconds of the regulation game time. Boise State, as the underdog, had been leading the game 28-10 with 5:16 remaining in the third quarter. The tide turned when an Oklahoma punt took a crazy bounce and careened off the leg of a Boise State player. Twenty-five unanswered points later, Oklahoma led 35-28. Now Boise State was facing a fourth down and 18 yards to go at mid-field, with 18 seconds left. Earlier in the game, with 1:02 minutes remaining, Boise State's quarterback had thrown an interception allowing Oklahoma to score a touchdown that put them seven points ahead. Even though it seemed that he had just thrown away the biggest game of his career with one bad decision, he had

Perseverance

learned to dismiss negative thoughts and stay in a positive frame of mind. But, two incomplete passes later, Boise State faced fourth down and 18 once again, at mid-field, fifty yards from the end zone. Imagine having any sense of hope when you are fifty yards away from the end zone, and you have to make 18 yards in just one play or it is over. Boise State still believed, and decided to go with a play called "circus." Their quarterback threw a 15-yard pass to the wide receiver, who caught it on Oklahoma's 35-yard line. He then turned and pitched the ball to a running back who raced into the end zone. With only seven seconds left to play, Boise State tied the game! The decision was made to kick the extra point and take their chances in overtime, instead of trying to end the game then and there by going for a two-point conversion. At first, this didn't seem like a good decision. Oklahoma scored on their first play in overtime to make the score 42-35. Boise State got the ball and, after six failed plays, they were facing fourth and two from the five-yard line. Again, Boise State called the circus play where the quarterback was a decoy and the ball was hiked to a 5'9" utility player who had not thrown a pass all season. The pass was perfect and again Boise State had the decision to tie the game with an extra point or go for the win by making a two-point conversion. Boise State decided to go for the two points to try to win. Using another trick play, the quarterback fooled the defense with a fake throw and then, with the opposite hand, the quarterback snuck the ball behind him where a running back grabbed it and headed for the end zone, scoring two points to win the game. Even though it was very late, I was so wound up after that finish that there was no way I could turn off the lights, go to bed and sleep!

   My first emotion was that I had given up on Boise State ever winning that game and I was disappointed in myself

The Transition

for not having hope, staying positive and persevering. I started thinking about recent events in my life where I had "pulled the horse back in midstream" instead of moving ahead with plans that I wanted to implement. I was excited about the lesson this football game had taught me – that, through perseverance, miracles do happen! Even though I had not always succeeded in persevering in the past, now I had new hope and I knew not to stop midstream. I knew I would have the courage and the perseverance to forge ahead.

Positive people already know what negative people need to understand – that past behavior doesn't have to dictate how we deal with future problems. We must always put aside past defeats and, by doing so, we will understand that not only does each new day bring a new challenge, but that with that challenge comes new results based on the choices we make and the approach we take to deal with the resolution of new problems. I have adopted a mantra that helps me in the way I approach resolving problems: you can't change the past, but you can ruin today by worrying about tomorrow. Disregarding things not in my control, I start each day by facing each new situation with the statement, "The only unknown in life is today. Yesterday is known and tomorrow depends on decisions made today!"

To persevere you need to have self-discipline, remain focused on your main objective and be patient until things finally work out. This means you are in continual action, handling disappointment, frustration or even massive rejection. Those who are believers and who persevere know they cannot afford to let up, that victory is still within their grasp even though the scoreboard shows they are behind. Doesn't this football game epitomize all the definitions of perseverance? I always keep this game in mind when I start thinking there is too little time left and no way to recover.

Perseverance

Perseverance is the most essential trait necessary to overcome adversity, but I have to mention how difficult it is to persevere though a negative time. We are all different, whether heredity or environmental influences have shaped our lives. Why do some people seem to worry more than others? Why do certain people have nerves of steel and plenty of confidence? Whether shy or bold, none of us has an excuse not to persevere through an adversity. Yes, it will be easier for some than for others, but perseverance is not about easy. It is about having the desire, the plan and the motivation to carry on in the face of adversity. It all comes down to this – I believe and I will not accept anything less. Why do we stop trying during trying times? Clare Booth Luce once said, "There are no hopeless situations; there are only men who have grown hopeless about them."

In most cases, hopelessness develops when we are overwhelmed. It's difficult to think clearly and easy to lose hope when facing an overwhelming event. When I have dealt with long-term adversities, I found I was overwhelmed by the complexity of the event or the length of time it would take to resolve. As a result, my plan is now to break the issue down into segments. It is easier to deal with the individual parts, enabling you to persevere for the long term.

How do you break the problem down into smaller parts? The best way to explain this technique is to share a story with you about my father-in-law. It is truly a story of overcoming a long-term adversity, using both perseverance and a positive mental attitude. At age 59, he underwent open-heart surgery at the Mayo Clinic, required due to clogged arteries leading to his heart. The surgery was successful but, within a year's time, his arteries had become clogged again. He then had a second surgery but again his arteries clogged. He consulted with

The Transition

the doctors at the Mayo Clinic and was informed that because of the severity of his condition, he was not a good candidate for another heart surgery. One can only imagine how overwhelmed he felt and how easy it would have been for him to lose hope. In 1976, not many other options were offered to heart patients who could not undergo another operation. The doctor's verdict was often regarded as a death sentence. This adverse event had not only changed his life but also threatened to take it. It might seem that adversity of this magnitude could not be broken down into manageable parts. No one would be surprised to find someone facing this to think that way. But remember, it is the perseverance time frame, and not the adversity, that we divide into segments. Instead of giving up and losing hope, my father-in-law and his wife found an article in the Wall Street Journal, explaining how a person could change his diet and increase his longevity. The article featured the Pritikin Longevity Center in Santa Monica, California. Feeling this was his only hope, my father-in-law signed up for a month's stay at Pritikin to learn how to select and cook certain foods for a healthier lifestyle. Once on his new diet, he began to feel more energetic. He established a number of goals and set timetables in order to appreciate small victories as he moved forward over the hurdles life had placed in his path. The adversity remained, as did the perseverance. In addition to his diet, he improved his health by walking two miles every day. For a number of years, he would walk the entire 18 holes when he golfed. He set his mind to this, even though his golfing partners rode in their carts. Approaching age 80, he knew this was good for his health. By persevering using exercise and diet, he was able to stay healthy and live another 24 years beyond his first open heart surgery. The small victories along the way

Perseverance

created the ultimate win. I believe Walter Elliot said it best, "Perseverance is not a long race; it is many short races, one after another."

My father-in-law's health situation is a perfect example of what can be achieved when you list the steps that need to be taken to restore happiness in your life, with a timetable of how long to allow for each step to be completed. There is an additional element. Do not give up when encountering roadblocks on your pathway to victory. You may feel as if you have been defeated in your quest unless you treat the roadblocks as only temporary setbacks.

As you proceed in accomplishing your goals according to the timetable you set for yourself, there will be moments when you will be convinced that there is no way you can go on. You may feel physically exhausted, emotionally distraught, or both, resulting in daily depression. It is at this time that you must have faith and understand that perseverance may take the path of a rollercoaster. Setbacks are common and to be expected. On your list of written goals, be sure to use red ink when writing these words: "I understand that there will be setbacks and I truly believe they are only temporary."

Let me share with you a time when I felt like I could no longer persevere. I was ready to accept defeat. During that period, I didn't fully understand that setbacks could be temporary nor did I understand that those setbacks came from sources outside me as well as from within.

My wife and I were invited to celebrate the 50th birthday of a close friend. The party boarded a double-decker bus and headed to a renowned Jazz club located in a then seedy section of downtown Denver. This area has since been redeveloped but, at the time, it was filled with warehouses and loading docks – a hang-out for alcoholics, transients and the homeless.

The Transition

I was very depressed. I had been waging a two-year battle in federal court. I was countersuing The Resolution Trust Corporation for its actions regarding the Savings and Loan crisis. This situation had devastated my business and my family's financial security. I felt no party spirit so I stepped out of the bar into the alley to be alone with my thoughts.

Across the alley, a pair of eyes stared at me out of the darkness from under a loading dock. As the man came out from under the dock, he approached me, staggering as he walked. I realized from the long jet black hair to the red headband he wore around it, that he was an American Indian. An ungenerous thought occurred to me – that, while I had had troubles before, they may be about to get a lot worse.

The man stopped in front of me and asked if I would give him two dollars. I was in a terrible and righteous frame of mind just then, so I responded indignantly by telling him that, if he had any pride, he would not resort to begging and would at least offer something in exchange for the money.

He stared at me for a moment, then reached into his pocket and pulled out a knife. I remember clearly thinking, "Dennis, how stupid are you that you are attempting to teach a lesson in an alley in downtown Denver late at night?!" The man then pushed the knife toward me and it was then that he offered to trade me the knife for the two dollars. My good sense was again overtaken by my mood as I told him that he wasn't very bright if he was trading a knife clearly worth ten dollars for two. After my utterance, clarity hit me at the possibility of losing all my money, and more, at the point of his knife, so I tried to diffuse the damage of what I had said to him. I asked him what he thought about as he tried to fall asleep under that dock. His face lit up as he told me about his wife and month old child.

Perseverance

He had been laid off from the mines in Meeker, Colorado, and had come to Denver to earn money for his family. Pushing further, I asked him about his dreams.

Looking upward, he told me he dreamed about being the man who owned the tall skyscraper behind me. I told him that I had to appear in federal court to save ownership of *my* buildings, and thinking once again of my own problems, I complained that after years of hard work, I had to sell everything I owned to avoid bankruptcy.

Then I handed him a ten dollar bill and he held out the knife, but, when I reached for it, he didn't release it. I chastised myself yet again for being so stupid, anticipating what I thought would happen next.

But he looked at me, with sincerity reflecting in his dark eyes, and he said, "After meeting me, do you see that your problems are not that bad?" He released the knife and disappeared back under the loading dock. His simple comment had put my thoughts into perspective. With tears in my eyes, but feeling energized, I vowed to persevere and to return to federal court the following day with the motto, "I will win!"

Chapter Seven
Organization and Goals – The Great Equalizers

ORGANIZATION

Organization can be used as a tool to assist a person in becoming successful in whatever endeavor he or she chooses, whether in business or in other facets of life. It can be that extra help used to overcome other deficiencies in our lives, such as lack of education. It can put you on equal footing with competitors. A person who is well organized can compete and win against those people who have better natural skills or skills that have been attained through specialized, higher education. But how is organization applicable when transitioning to the 4th quarter of life?

It is well known that, as we age, our motor and mental

The Transition

skills diminish in capacity. It seems like we are not quite as lively, energetic or mentally agile as we once were. Even though Boomers offer great wisdom and experience, certain companies feel they need to hire younger workers, phasing out the older workforce. With the advent of the cyber world and increasing technology, the older of the Boomers have an even greater disadvantage since they did not grow up using computers and the Internet.

An important tool in getting organized and feeling good about yourself for doing it is making a daily, *written* "To Do" list. Not only do you become more productive, but you achieve satisfaction when you see the progress of checking off each item for the day. As you become more productive, you can actually look forward to writing the "To Do" list for the next day. Another important benefit in writing your list is that, by putting your thoughts on paper, the result is reduced mental stress and clutter. You become excited about making your list each day, accomplishing the items and achieving the mental freedom these accomplishments bring.

A written "To Do" list will help you maintain control over your life by protecting your personal time and making sure you understand that you are a priority. When we don't make ourselves a priority, we spend most of our time each day taking care of little tasks, never quite accomplishing the large and important items. There is seldom time left for those important items, or for yourself. The best example of this is epitomized by using the "Rocks in a Jar" philosophy.

If you have a pile of sand (small tasks), medium rocks (essential items to do), and large rocks (major projects) in front of you, when you put them all in a jar (your daily routine), you leave only one way that things can be accomplished. If you spend all your time filling the jar with sand and medium rocks, there is no way the large rocks will

Organization and Goals – The Great Equalizers

fit in the jar. However, if you put the large rocks in the jar first, then add the medium rocks to fit in the smaller openings, the sand you add will pour in and around all the rocks to fill the jar. You must learn to accomplish major tasks first. Prioritizing free time for yourself is a major task and a priority. We often don't leave enough time to accomplish the major items and, as a result, there is no free time for you.

Once a person starts using the written "To Do" list as one of the tools in the organization plan, he or she will be ready to write goals and a game plan for the 4th quarter. In looking at my daily list, I saw that I was accomplishing all the minor items, but not protecting my personal time. It was necessary to change my game plan and re-evaluate my personal objectives before writing my goals for the new year. I decided that I needed to take my age into consideration, along with cash flow/net worth and *changing* personal interests.

One of the biggest mistakes you can make, whether it is evaluating the stock market or in your personal decision-making process, is to delay decisions and actions when the past is no longer applicable. When re-evaluating your personal objectives, it is imperative to slow down and take a good look around. You need to relax and change routines in order to create freshness and to keep an open mind. Maybe for the first time, you need to be aware of your own needs, rather than the needs others have chosen for you. You need to take control by letting others know what you will and won't participate in.

Since change can be so difficult, one of my year's goal sheets is entitled "Adjusting to Change." I had spent a year "flexing down" in my business career. As a result of flexing (or slowing) down, many changes occurred in my life. They were major changes, making the adjustment quite difficult.

The Transition

Because of this, I found it hard to change routines and to get comfortable with things changing in my life. Instead of approaching change as negative, I chose to welcome it and even get excited about it. I was determined to be open to change and to let it create that freshness in my life.

GOALS

Having goals as you transition into the 4th quarter of life is more important than ever before. Earlier in our lives, we could make more corrections, change course more often and barely be affected. This is no longer the case, and it is very important to stay with a pre-conceived plan in order to accomplish all of your goals. To take side roads and detours will lead to negative consequences and disappointment.

Goals, as on your "To Do" list, should *always* be in writing. If they aren't, they are no more than a dream. You may know what you want out of life, but now you need to take the time to draw up a plan in order to achieve it. Organization *requires* a plan. The plan provides focus. Once you are focused, you will be able to visualize your goals, making them sharp, specific and well defined. Okay – how do you put your goals together? Do you write them out like you do your New Year's resolutions? Do you type them out (in large print!) and post them on the vanity mirror or the refrigerator door? Do you try to memorize them? Should you share them with others?

Goals must be written and must be specific, yet allow for flexibility. They are a roadmap as they not only chart your course, but also find the shortest possible route to your destination. Goals and a plan are vital. If you don't know where you are going, you end up lost!

Organization and Goals – The Great Equalizers

If you would like to post your New Year's resolutions on your mirror, that is fine. But, when goals are written out, their format doesn't easily allow for them to be posted like a single quip, quote or positive affirmation. Written goals will be more like a coach's playbook. Memorizing them may be too difficult. Sharing them with others is valuable only if you are certain you have the positive support in your goals from those you choose to tell. Written goals provide a needed progress report because you then must set deadlines for accomplishing different things.

Goals should reflect your wants, needs and desires. And, as you transition into the 4th quarter of your life, one additional item must be added. To achieve the happiness and satisfaction you are seeking, your goals need to be your own, and not goals dictated by others in your life.

I promised this book would be different than other books in that it would provide tools to assist you, instead of just providing positive "rah rah" thoughts and suggestions. I have saved my annual goals for the past 33 years. I believe goals should be written on an annual basis, following the calendar year.

Every year, after the holidays, I find nothing more satisfying than to sit down in the sometimes tedious days of January to write my goals. You're probably thinking, "This guy needs to get a life!" But my life has been filled with much excitement and even daring moments.

Goals provide a positive outlook on life. The most excitement we ever experience is the anticipation of looking forward. Remember the excitement of earning a good grade after you had studied so hard for it? Remember the anticipation of that special trip you had planned for years to take? Think of the excitement you felt when things were going so well that you thought you must be dreaming. Your goals are all about you and the positive things that

The Transition

will happen when your written plans come true. What could be more exciting than having your highest expectations met?

The only way goals can be effective is to use a technique that also involves objectives and strategy. Goals, objective and strategy join together to create a plan that can be accomplished and implemented.

Goals are automatically met when you achieve all of your annual objectives. To achieve the objectives, you need to write down defined strategies. This is where the details come in. These strategies set everything into action and with the success of that action, the listed objectives are accomplished. For many years, people have said to me, "Automatic sounds like you don't have to work on your goals" and "Aren't goals and objectives the same thing?" They are not. Your goal or master plan is actually the one item that you want to accomplish. Your objectives are multiple items that you set into action and, upon completion of these items, your goal automatically becomes accomplished. For these objectives to be completed, a person must write out and use defined strategies. Strategies are very detailed and provide flexibility. I personally like to apply priorities to each and every one. So, as you now can see, it is a stepping-stone process whereby working on the strategies sets everything into action, and success of that action accomplishes the listed objective. If and when all the objectives are accomplished, the goal is met.

An example of one of my master plans follows. It will show a way of laying out your goals, objectives and strategies. We will review the plan, beginning at the base. You will see why flexibility is necessary in the strategies at the base of the plan, while the objectives and goals remain steadfast. This has confused people who then ask me how I can write my entire master plan (often in excess of ten pages) in January and project forward into the coming year. I have always done it this way and it works because I am flexible on strategies, not the goal and objectives. Every Monday morning, you need to review your strategies and lay out the game plan for the coming week. I have always appreciated this quote: "A dream is what you would *like* for life to be and to hold, but a goal is what you *intend* to make happen."

EXAMPLE

MASTER PLAN

GOALS

    1. PERSONAL:

        a. To not take my physical health for granted. To take the proper steps to plan for the long run of my health.

        b. To learn to know myself and to learn to be myself. To learn how to be happy with an environment I build myself.

        c. To assist people in emotional or financial need.

    2. BUSINESS:

        a. To keep my company open for business and

The Transition

        write-offs.
- b. To create a new investment portfolio for retirement.
- c. To consult as a hospital board director.

OBJECTIVES

1. To feel better physically and to assist my mental and emotional health, I will (one step at a time):

   a. Exercise daily.

   b. Set the guidelines for my environment. The more decisive I am, the clearer the picture of who I want to be.

2. To collect notes receivable and bonuses.

3. To help improve patient safety in hospitals by serving on a national level.

STRATEGIES

(Methods used to achieve the objectives and meet the goal – see "Goals and Priorities")

Behavior is the key to success. If I modify my behavior, I can change my results.

To accomplish my master plan, I must set into action and accomplish the following list by using the following defined strategies:

Organization and Goals – The Great Equalizers

1. My Life, Body and Mind:

    a. To be aware of my own needs, rather than those inspired by others.

    b. To make exercise enjoyable and a part of every day.

    c. To find and be my true self so that I can hold and enjoy the greatest treasures: peace of mind and freedom.

    d. To look forward with anticipation to running a new race and to win, instead of leaning back to rest on my laurels.

    e. To accomplish my personal plans:

    - In order to feel better physically and to assert my mental and emotional health, I will exercise (join a gym) and work only six hours a day, golfing on Tuesdays.

    - Golf – practice and stretch by going to a driving range two days a week; play twice a week.

    - Speak to people who have lost hope by visiting shelters and other locations.

    - Volunteer time at the Denver Rescue Mission.

    - Travel – to Ireland, China and Greece; in

The Transition

winter, Hawaii, Scottsdale.

- Develop and cook special recipes (green chile, wing sauce, red Italian sauce, clam chowder, sloppy joes).

2. Continue to keep my company open for business for the following reasons:

    a. Broker's license

    b. Depreciate vehicles

    c. Health insurance

3. Decide how to invest during the transition period:

    a. Use a wealth management company.

    b. Consider under-valued blue chip stocks with high dividend yields.

    c. Invest in a secure income property, without liability or risk, to create a long-term monthly income with capital appreciation.

    d. Keep liquid with two years' of cash (CDs, Money Market Funds) on hand to pay expenses.

Organization and Goals – The Great Equalizers

I AM A PERSON WHO NEEDS POSITIVE AFFIRMATIONS.

In all my studies, I have not encountered any philosophies that have inspired me more than Thoreau, Emerson and Napoleon Hill. Their insights and reflections will be my guideposts through my life. Their words follow:

"Without knowing yourself and being yourself, you cannot truly use the one Great Secret that gives you power to mold your future and make life carry you the way you want to go."

"Only the man who has found his true self can know himself, find his own best talents and achieve his own high success."

"One good way to maintain possession of your own mind and to allow others to possess their own minds is to keep certain views to yourself. You are not required to go through life explaining yourself."

"To be free is a great gift. To achieve that, you do not need great amounts of money or influence or power. All you need is the ability to place yourself in a non-confrontive mode. First with yourself, and second with the world around you."

Using my master plan as a guide, I hope you now will use this format and fill in the strategies, objectives and priorities in order to meet your goals. As my example shows, my basic premises and goals have changed from previous quarters of my life, yet the new premises and goals are equally exciting.

Chapter Eight
Your Best Health in the 4th Quarter

By Lawrence Emmons, M.D.,Ph.D.

Perhaps you have seen a football team gather on the sidelines between the 3rd and 4th quarter. They join their left hands and raise their right hands, extending four fingers, clenching their fists or raising their helmets. What is the significance of this gesture? It's a signal to the other team and to themselves that they "own" the 4th quarter; that they have prepared themselves in every possible way to perform at their peak. It is important that people who are transitioning into the 4th quarter be focused on maximizing their physical health so that they have the best opportunity to win the game.

You may be in the best physical condition of your life. If you are, that's great. But more than likely you're not and there are a few good reasons why. If you want to be able to

The Transition

take advantage of opportunities and really enjoy the 4th quarter, you should consider following a few principles I will outline in this chapter.

First, I'd like to provide a few definitions. According to Miriam-Webster, "*Health* is the condition of being sound in mind, body and spirit," or it can be "the general condition of the body." You could say that you are in good health or poor health. *Wellness,* on the other hand, is always "the quality or state of being in good health." *Aging* is the process of growing older and undergoing the biological effects that growing older entails. If you're talking about wine, it means mellowing or ripening. That is probably the most positive way to think about what happens to all humans as the years go by.

Generally, we should be at peak physical condition in our second quarter. Strength and endurance are at their theoretical maximum and the cells that make up our bodies are performing at their best. As time goes by, cells become less effective at repairing themselves and doing the jobs for which they were designed. They may be injured by outside assaults such as smoking or a poor diet. They may be injured by trauma or inflammation. The relative health of some cells is strongly influenced by genetic factors. All these factors are the reasons why you are probably not in the best state of health as you enter the 4th quarter. You may not be able to regain the endurance, strength and flexibility that you had when you were 30, but by following a few principles, you can slow down or even reverse the aging process.

Literally thousands of books and articles have been written about achieving and maintaining optimum health. There are thousands of websites entirely devoted to wellness issues. It would be a daunting task to read and understand even a small fraction of the information that is available. In fact, the conclusions of as many as one half of these research articles are subsequently refuted. So, even if you could keep up with all the books and articles that are published, much of what you would be learning would be incorrect. Rather than inundate you with information, I would prefer to present a few principles that, if followed, will help you achieve your maximum health.

Principle #1: There is synergy to be gained in efforts to achieve good health.

For example, if you are successful in losing weight, you are more likely to exercise because you look better, feel better and it's easier to do. If you exercise more, you are more likely to lose weight and your blood pressure will probably decrease. If you stop smoking, you may be able to exercise more easily and you will reduce your risk of lung cancer or COPD (Chronic Obstructive Pulmonary Disease).

The combined effect of working in two or more areas is greater than the sum of their individual effects. Therefore, it is more effective to make several changes in your lifestyle at once rather than to just, for example, try to lose 10 pounds or go to the gym to work out three times a week. Both are excellent goals but the results will be suboptimal and may take so long that…well, remember that we are talking about the 4th quarter here.

Principle #2: Have a knowledgeable, caring, friendly physician and make him or her a part of your personal advisory board.

Isn't it great when you can call a trusted mechanic

The Transition

whenever you have a concern or question about your car? I've owned a number of Audi automobiles over the years. They have been great cars. But the best part of owning them has been the fact that I have a "Certified Audi Mechanic" as a trusted friend. He has saved me untold dollars, time and grief in dealing with my cars. He knows when things are about to go wrong with a car. He knows the family history of Audis and what part is likely to fail at what time. He knows when a problem needs to be fixed and when it can be watched, and he understands me well enough to know how to explain problems and their potential solutions to me. He has even "prescribed" remedies for my car when it is in another part of the world.

If you don't already have one, make every effort to find a physician who can do the same for you as my mechanic does for my car. You want someone who will take the time to learn and understand your medical issues including your family history, underlying health problems, previous diseases or injuries, your habits and current state of health. You want that person to be able to explain to you what to watch for as you age. You want him to be proactive in ordering protective screening studies.

You want your physician to be available to explain medical issues to you. He doesn't need to be an expert in every area of medicine, but he should be able to interpret medical terminology for you and serve as your protector should you have a serious medical problem and require hospitalization or a procedure.

There are concierge or retainer physician practices that provide this type of service for a fixed annual fee or you can discuss a similar arrangement with an internist or family practice physician on a fee-for-service basis. If you are having trouble finding the right primary care practitioner for you but have a friend who is a physician

Your Best Health in the 4th Quarter

of another specialty or possibly a nurse who works in a hospital, ask for a referral to someone who they know and trust.

Principle #3: Pay attention to your diet.

There is evidence that by simply reducing the amount of food you eat you may significantly decrease your risk of developing diabetes, hypertension and cancer, and reduce your risk of heart attack and stroke, resulting in a longer lifespan. This is especially true if you are significantly overweight. In addition, weight loss will make you feel and look better. It will reduce stress on your bones and joints and make it easier for you to be active.

Your weight is like a bank account, only this bank account is one that you want to optimize at the right amount rather than maximize. It is a running balance between calories out and calories in. The number of calories in is the total amount of energy taken in as food and beverages, and the number of calories out is the amount of energy your body expends in performing normal body functions and physical activity. If you take in more calories than you spend, you will add to your account, i.e. your weight. If you spend more calories than you take in, you will lose weight. If intake equals expenditure, your weight will be stable.

If you are like me, you grew up in a home where the mantra was "Eat everything on your plate. Remember the poor people in...*fill in the blank.*" Or "Have another donut. We have loads." The secret to reducing calorie intake if weight loss or weight stabilization is your goal is "**don't** eat everything on your plate", "**don't** fill up your plate" and "**don't** have another donut." If you remember that a can of

The Transition

cola contains 143 calories (of sugar) and that by drinking that cola you condemn yourself to an extra 8 minutes of swimming or 15 minutes of cycling to burn those calories, you may decide to drink water instead. Your decision to drink water may also be influenced by the fact that 3500 extra calories ingested translates to one extra pound of weight. One extra can of cola each day will result in a weight gain of 15 pounds per year unless you increase your activity level to burn those extra calories.

Not only should you consider reducing your calorie input by reducing portions and not taking in unnecessary calories (that extra cola each day), but you should pay attention to the quality of the food you eat and when you eat it. Focus on foods that are high in vitamins, minerals and fiber, and low in saturated and hydrogenated fats and simple sugars. Certain foods are known to be particularly beneficial to your health and you should go out of your way to include them in your diet. These include spinach, carrots, oats, blueberries, yogurt, tomatoes, walnuts and black beans.

Timing of meals is important and starts with breakfast. Don't skip it. Remember, at 8 a.m. you probably haven't had anything to eat in the previous twelve hours. A nutritious breakfast, even if just a few hundred calories, will improve your attitude, concentration and alertness, and will make you feel better. It will also start your daily eating pattern off on the right foot. That pattern might be based on six light meals during the day beginning with a substantial breakfast and followed by a midmorning snack, light lunch, mid-afternoon snack, light dinner and an evening snack. This meal pattern is thought to increase your overall metabolism leading to greater weight loss for the number of calories ingested. It will decrease your craving for large calorie "fixes." This eating pattern reduces the tendency toward insulin resistance which can lead to Type II diabetes and it has been shown to reduce cholesterol levels, especially LDL (bad) cholesterol levels.

Information and details on improving your diet are available from hundreds of sources. Some of the best information can be found on the following websites: www.release.com; www.eatright.org (American Dietetic Association); www.mypyramid.gov (United States Department of Agriculture.)

Principle #4: Exercise regularly.

"Use it or lose it." That's great advice and accurate, too. A 2006 study showed that Americans who exercised the equivalent of walking 30 minutes a day for five days a week lived 1.3 to 1.5 years longer on average than those who are less active. And if you run instead of walk for 30 minutes a day five days a week, you extend your life on average 3.5 to 3.7 years. People who don't start exercising until later can still add years to their lives and feel better in the process.

Positive effects of exercise contributing to increased longevity include weight loss, improved bone density, reduced injuries, reduced blood pressure, improved sleep, improved brain function, reduced risk of diabetes and reduced risk of heart disease.

A combination of aerobic exercise three to five times each week and resistance training two to three times each week is probably ideal to achieve maximum benefits. Aerobic exercise such as running, swimming or cycling increases the efficiency of oxygen use giving us better endurance, strength and calorie burn. Even slow-paced jogging for 30 minutes can burn 300 calories. If you do this five times each week for a year, that amounts to 22 pounds

The Transition

per year in reduced weight (at 3500 calories per pound) and, once you lose weight, aerobic exercise helps to keep it off.

Resistance training is effort expended against an opposing force for the purpose of developing the strength and size of skeletal muscles. Besides improving the way you look in a swimming suit, business suit or your birthday suit, resistance training makes maintaining your weight easier because muscle burns more calories than fat does. This is particularly important in the 4th quarter when muscle mass and metabolism are in decline. Resistance training improves mobility and flexibility which are especially important in the 4th quarter.

If you don't already invest in an exercise program, now is the time to begin. The benefits are too great to ignore any longer. It's a good idea to let your doctor know what you plan to do. Once cleared by the doctor, getting started can be as simple as going for a brisk walk several times a week. Walk long enough and fast enough to increase your breathing and heart rate. You should still be able to carry on a conversation.

Resistance training can also begin simply. Just set aside 30 minutes three times per week. You can begin by using milk bottles filled with sand or water as barbells, or using elastic cords. There are many books, articles and websites that describe exercise plans, but the most efficient and effective way to get started is to have a session with a professional fitness advisor who will formulate an exercise plan specifically for you and show you how to do the exercises properly.

Your Best Health in the 4th Quarter

Principle #5: Practice preventive maintenance and early detection.

Just as an airplane is required to have annual servicing during which the engine and flight controls are thoroughly checked for wear and impending failure, you should also be sure to have certain tests done on a regular basis.

The annual checkup with a physician has been a tradition in America for nearly 100 years. Approximately 20% of adults get a preventive physical examination every year. The usefulness of the annual exam has been debated for as long as they have been done and no major health organization recommends them. I believe there are two reasons to have a routine physical examination and neither involve being physically examined.

One is to build the doctor-patient relationship as noted in Principle #2 above. It is a good time to talk about any concerns or questions that you may have and for your doctor to talk to you about any concerns for your health given his knowledge about you.

The second reason for visiting a physician annually is that it gives your doctor the opportunity to discuss with you any tests that he believes should be done and why. Some of these tests can be done in the office and others may require visits to specialists. Let me give a few examples of tests that you and your physician may wish to consider.

A blood pressure measurement every year can be done in your doctor's office or in your neighborhood drug store. A blood glucose test every three years and a cholesterol blood test every five years can be done in your doctor's office or by prescription at a local laboratory.

There are some tests which have been shown statistically to improve longevity. There are several tests, however, which have not been shown to be effective and

The Transition

which might actually cause you harm by resulting in a "false positive" finding which leads to more tests or pins an incorrect diagnosis on you. These include whole body CT scans and routine annual chest x-rays.

Whole body CT scanning has been available for a few years and is touted by some as a method for early detection of disease in people with no symptoms. There is no data to suggest that whole body CT scanning is advantageous and, in fact, the x-ray exposure from these scans could actually increase your chances of developing cancer. They also frequently result in the discovery of findings that require follow-up but are ultimately of no significance.

An estimated 52,000 people died from colorectal carcinoma in the United States in 2007. This number could have been substantially reduced with colon screening. Colonoscopy should be performed at age 50 and every ten years thereafter in the average risk person, and earlier and more frequently in high risk people who, for example, have a family or personal history of colon cancer or polyps. Traditional colonoscopy using a long tube with a camera on the end can be used and the American Cancer Society has recently sanctioned virtual colonoscopy as a screening tool. Virtual colonoscopy is a radiologic procedure performed on a CT scanner after appropriate bowel preparation. It avoids the mechanical trauma and sedation of traditional colonoscopy but does expose you to radiation.

Coronary artery CT is a relatively new procedure that uses a CT scanner to directly visualize the arteries that supply blood to the heart. It shows great promise and is currently used to evaluate the coronary arteries in some symptomatic or high-risk patients, but it is not yet routinely used for screening. X-ray exposure is relatively high with this examination and the study requires medication to slow the heart rate. It must be performed on a high resolution CT

Your Best Health in the 4th Quarter

scanner using advanced analysis software and interpreted by a radiologist or cardiologist with special training. Talk to your physician about whether you should undergo this procedure.

If you are a woman, it is a good idea to have a DEXA scan when you reach menopause. A DEXA scan measures bone density in the lumbar spine and hip, and is highly correlated with fracture risk. It can signal to your physician that lifestyle changes are in order to try and build up bone density. These changes might include stretching exercises or weight training. Medications might be prescribed to increase bone mass and your physician might investigate for the presence of thyroid disease or arthritis which could predispose to osteoporosis. The increased risk of fracture as a result of osteoporosis is very significant and there is a high correlation between hip fracture and mortality within one year.

The risk of osteoporosis is not limited to women. A man with osteoporosis is more likely to sustain fractures and also has an increased mortality rate. If you are a man who has sustained a fracture with relatively minor trauma or who has lost height, you should also consider a DEXA scan.

Mammography is a screening test for breast cancer that should first be performed at age 40 and then annually thereafter unless you are at high risk for breast cancer, in which case screening should begin earlier. Mammographic screening has been shown to reduce the mortality from breast cancer and should be done in conjunction with periodic breast exams.

The Pap Test or Papanicolaou Smear has been in existence since the 1920s and data indicating its efficacy first appeared in the 1960s. It has been shown to reduce the incidence and mortality from cancer of the cervix by at

The Transition

least 80% in younger women. However, in women over age 60 who have had negative Pap tests, it is of minimal value and is not useful in women who have had a hysterectomy with removal of the cervix for a benign condition.

An annual dental exam is recommended with careful attention to the condition of the teeth, gums, fit of dentures and soft tissues for oral lesions. Similarly, an eye examination every one to two years should be done. Many eye conditions have no obvious symptoms. Vision changes routinely occur during the 40s and 50s. Conditions such as hypertension and diabetes can effect the eyes as well as cataracts, macular degeneration and glaucoma. Early detection of these conditions can save your vision.

The value of PSA measurements for prostate cancer is still being assessed, as is routine dermatologic screening for skin cancer.

It is very important to practice your own preventive maintenance and early detection programs. Don't depend on your doctor to discover an abnormality when you already know there may be a problem. Pay attention to what your body is telling you. If you have a new skin lesion or a mole that is changing in appearance, report it to your doctor. If you notice a suspicious breast lump, report it. Ignoring issues generally won't make them go away.

Principle #6: Maximize your good habits and eliminate the bad ones.

We all know that the use of tobacco products is bad for your health. Don't smoke! Don't chew tobacco! Chewing increases your risk of oral cancer several fold. Smoking increases your risk of lung cancer by a factor of 22 if you are a man and 12 if you are a woman. Twenty thousand more

Your Best Health in the 4th Quarter

women die every year from lung cancer than from breast cancer. Smoking increases your risk of emphysema by a factor of ten and increases your risk of death from heart disease by a factor of three. It increases your risk of oral cancer, esophageal cancer, stomach cancer and bladder cancer.

Smoking decreases the ability of your lungs to exchange oxygen between the air you inhale and your blood, making it more difficult to exercise or even do every day activities.

Within one year of quitting, your risk of heart disease decreases by one-half. Within 5 to 15 years, your risk of stroke decreases to equal that of people who have never smoked. At ten years, your risk of lung cancer decreases by one-half from that of smokers. If you smoke, get help starting a smoking cessation program. Your physician can recommend a program and prescribe medications that can ease the transition to non-smoker.

Alcohol is a double-edged sword. If you don't have problem with alcohol addiction, one or two drinks per night can reduce your blood pressure and raise your HDL levels which can have a beneficial effect on your heart. It may reduce your risk of heart disease by as much as 50 to 60%. The National Institute of Alcohol Abuse and Alcoholism reported that moderate drinkers live longer than non-drinkers or heavy drinkers. Many studies from around the world have confirmed that moderate drinkers have a significantly reduced mortality compared to abstainers or heavy drinkers. Some studies have shown that moderate drinkers are less likely to develop diabetes. Many studies have shown a decreased risk for Alzheimers disease among moderate drinkers.

Obviously, if you are a recovering alcoholic, react adversely to alcohol or have been warned against drinking alcohol by your doctor, you should abstain. Too much alcohol consumption will decrease your life expectancy, especially if you mix drinking and driving.

Dental floss has been used since prehistoric times and you should use it too. It cleans up to 30% of the surface of your teeth that is missed with a toothbrush mainly between the teeth and along the gum margins. It will help you keep your teeth, give you fresher breath and avoid periodontal disease. There has been shown to be a strong link between gum disease and atherosclerosis possibly due to systemic inflammation or presence of bacteria that cause gum disease in the bloodstream. In any case, people with periodontal disease are nearly twice as likely to have coronary artery disease as those who have healthy gums and teeth. There may not be a causative connection between gum disease and heart disease, but even if there isn't, keeping your teeth and not having halitosis makes flossing every day a worthwhile endeavor.

Principle #7: Take a few supplements each day.

Men and women who take one baby aspirin a day have been shown to have a lower death rate overall, and from cardiovascular disease and cancer in particular, than those who don't. The overall decrease in death rate has been measured at 25%. The death rate from cardiovascular disease in women decreases almost 40%.

The improvement in mortality from cardiovascular disease is thought to stem from aspirin's antiplatelet effect which decreases the clotting ability of blood. Of course, this effect also can result in serious complications such as GI bleeding or bleeding in the brain and, therefore, aspirin therapy should only be started after discussions with your physician. Aspirin is an anti-inflammatory drug as well, and this may be the factor that can make it effective against malignancies and may have a hand in reducing arterial inflammation which has been implicated in heart attacks.

Clinical trials have shown that omega-3 fatty acid supplements can slow progression of atherosclerotic cardiovascular disease and reduce the incidence of strokes and heart attacks. They can reduce triglyceride levels, decrease blood pressure and decrease blood clotting. Omega-3 fatty acids are found mainly in fish such as salmon, mahi-mahi, tilapia or catfish. One to two grams per day of omega-3 supplement can also be taken.

Principle #8: Get 7 to 8 hours of sleep each night.

Poor sleep habits can be injurious to your health. If you sleep less than six hours per night, your odds of developing infections, hypertension, heart disease or stroke increase dramatically. The immediate effects of poor sleep include tiredness, weakness, difficulty concentrating and, in extreme cases, psychosis.

It is estimated that as many as 70% of Americans suffer from sleep problems, with these problems being more common in the 4th quarter of life.

Difficulty sleeping can be caused by physical problems such as chronic pain or heart disease which may cause night-time shortness of breath. It may be due to insomnia—a condition where you have trouble getting to sleep or going back to sleep after you wake. This is frequently caused by worrying or anxiety. It may be the result of sleep apnea which is caused by closure of the upper airway during sleep and leads to periods where you don't breathe for up to ten seconds, recovering with a start. Sleep apnea occurs most commonly in obese people. Restless legs

The Transition

syndrome can also cause sleep loss as a result of intermittent involuntary movement of the legs. Environmental issues such as noises (from a snoring partner) or the room temperature being too high can also impair your sleep.

Here are a few things you can try if you are having trouble getting quality sleep:

- Use your bed only for sleeping or sex
- Keep the TV out of your bedroom
- Don't eat, drink alcohol or caffeine, or exercise within two hours of bedtime
- Keep your bedroom cool and dark
- Add white noise from a fan or humidifier
- If you can't get to sleep, get up and read for awhile
- Invest in a good mattress since you will spend more time on your mattress than anywhere else
- Get into a rhythm by going to bed and getting up at the same time every day

If you are still having a difficult time sleeping, talk to your doctor about getting a formal sleep evaluation and possibly a prescription for a sleep aid.

Principle #9: Evaluate your medications.

You may be taking a medication for painful symptoms like an infection, allergies or gout. You are no doubt careful to take them for as long as prescribed, in the correct dosages and at the proper times. What is just as important are medications that you may require to deal with conditions which are not causing you symptoms now. In particular, hypertension and high cholesterol can and should be addressed, and if diet and exercise don't control them, medication is called for.

The risks of persistent high blood pressure are well-documented. Heart attack, stroke and peripheral vascular disease increase significantly. In fact, the increase is as much as 90 percent. You may be able to lower your blood pressure by as much as 20 mm with changes in lifestyle. If your blood pressure remains above 120/80 after decreasing your weight and improving your physical condition, then you should be taking medication to get your pressure into the safe range. Consult your physician to decide which medication or medications are best suited to you.

Statins are cholesterol lowering drugs. They particularly lower the LDL or "bad" component of cholesterol. Statins dramatically reduce incidence of heart attack and stroke…by as much as 50 percent. There is also accumulating evidence that statins may help in other disorders including osteoporosis, Alzheimer's disease and diabetes.

If your LDL cholesterol remains above 100 mg/dL and your total cholesterol remains above 200 mg/dL after aggressive changes in diet and exercise, you should consider taking a statin drug. In fact, a recent poll of cardiologists showed that 33 percent of them were taking a statin even though they had no risk factors for cardiovascular disease. Something to think about especially since side effects are rare.

Principle #10: Have faith.

Many scientific studies over the years have shown a positive relationship between spirituality and longevity. Some have argued that women tend to be more religious than men and since women have a higher life expectancy, one would expect that more spiritual people would live longer. Others have said that religious people have fewer bad habits than non-religious people. However, studies that factor out these issues still show that people who have religious faith have a lower mortality rate than those who don't. The *Handbook of Religion and Health* states that "Frequent religious attendance (once a week or more) is associated with a 25-33% reduction in the risk of dying during follow-up periods ranging from five to 28 years." Religiously active people tend to have less stress, healthier immune systems and fewer hospital admissions than others.

Principle #11: Reduce your stress level.

Stress is what your body and mind feel when confronted with outside or internal forces. Stress is always with us and is a normal part of lives, but when it is excessive and unrelenting, it can cause unpleasant physical symptoms such as headaches, stomach pains, sleep disruption and chest pains. It can also contribute to hypertension, heart disease, diabetes, asthma and skin conditions. It can affect your immune system, making you more susceptible to infections and cancer. Excessive stress also contributes to emotional disorders and makes you more likely to make mistakes and be involved in accidents.

The good news is that you are transitioning into the 4th quarter. You are starting to leave behind at least some of the major sources of stress. You probably are faced with fewer (or no) work-related frustrations and you have more time to deal with and complete unfinished tasks. On the other hand, major life events such as the death of a loved one, major illness, or a severe financial setback are still possible. In fact, if you have not suffered a significant loss of net worth recently, you are fortunate.

Using stress reduction techniques is important. Here are some things you can do to reduce stress:

- Exercise regularly
- Practice yoga
- Pray or meditate
- Practice positive self-affirmation
- Volunteer
- Make sure you keep a financial nest egg
- Use a "to do" list and a daily planner
- Keep a daily journal
- Join a support group
- Accept the fact that some things are beyond your control and focus on those things you can control. That is what this book is about.

If you are suffering from severe anxiety or depression, you should see a medical professional who can provide counseling and possibly medication to help relieve your symptoms and get you back on the road to positivity.

Summary

It is important to strive for your best health as you move into the 4th quarter. You can do this by having a trusted physician serving as your medical advisor and using his knowledge to make sure that you are properly screened and that chronic issues such as hypertension and

The Transition

hypercholesterolemia are dealt with. You should reach your optimum weight by improving your diet and exercise regimens. Make sure you get seven to eight hours of sleep each night and that you deal with stress properly. Add a few good habits and eliminate some bad ones.

Here are two checklists that you can follow and adjust to fit your needs. The first is a list of items to accomplish during the first month of your transition program, and the second is a daily to-do list to remind you to floss your teeth, take your aspirin, and other important activities.

FIRST MONTH "TO-DO" LIST:

- Find a physician to be your personal advisor if you don't already have one.

- Meet with your physician for a baseline examination and discussion about your general health.

- Measure a baseline blood pressure.

- Obtain baseline cholesterol blood tests.

- Establish a preventive maintenance schedule including mammography, colonoscopy, DEXA scanning, and eye examination.

- Begin a program to stop smoking if necessary.

- Moderate alcohol consumption.

Your Best Health in the 4th Quarter

- Formulate diet changes including calorie reduction and multiple meals.

- Formulate an exercise plan including aerobic and muscle-building.

- Evaluate your stress level and begin efforts to reduce it.

The Transition

DAILY "TO-DO" LIST:

- Diet
Calories _____ Meals _____

- Exercise
Aerobic _____ Muscle _____

- Floss
  _____

- Meds
Aspirin _____ Omega 3 _____
Statin _____ Blood Pressure _____

- Medication
  _____

- Sleep
7 to 8 hours _____

- Alcohol
1 to 2 glasses _____

- Pray or meditate

Your Best Health in the 4th Quarter

LAWRENCE L. EMMONS, M.D., Ph.D.
Diversified Radiology of Colorado
9395 Crown Crest Boulevard
Parker, Colorado 80138
(303) 269-4600

Dr. Emmons has been practicing medicine for 24 years and currently shares the responsibility in overseeing the operations of Diversified Radiology of Colorado, a group of 150 employees, including 50 radiologists. His education and experience includes:

Clinical/Research Interests:
Nuclear Medicine; CT and MR/Body Imaging; Emergency Radiology

Residency/Fellowship:
Presbyterian St. Luke's Medical Center, Denver, Colorado

Medical School:
University of Miami School of Medicine, Miami, Florida

Graduate School:
The University of Michigan, Ann Arbor, Michigan, M.S., Ph.D., Nuclear Engineering

Undergraduate School:
The University of Missouri, Columbia, Missouri, B.S., Physics

Chapter Nine
Tax Planning

By William R. Gougér, J.D., C.PA.

I have been practicing tax law for both business and individual clients since 1983. Being asked to write this important chapter for The Transition book was not only an honor but such good timing in that the Baby Boomers are now coming of age and beginning their transition into the 4th quarter of life. A perfect example of this is when author Dennis Niewoehner and his wife Marcia approached our firm with their transitioning questions. Dennis was just completing a 30-year career in real estate development and wanted to write this book as he transitioned into the 4th quarter. Changing careers is a major life event and he had many questions to be answered before feeling secure regarding this change. As a couple, Dennis & Marcia wanted to make sure that they knew the right steps to take

The Transition

before proceeding with actions that could cost them money in terms of higher income or estate taxes.

I would like to address seven specific areas related to taxes that people should focus on before taking action during the transitioning process.

Mortgages and Home Equity Loans

The 2008 national Financial Crisis has dramatically reduced real estate values, job security, investment portfolios, etc. One or more of these financial "hits" may have impacted your retirement/transition plans. Whatever impact you have suffered, however, you still need a place to live in. If you own your home (as a large majority of people do at this stage of their life), this particular topic is as relevant as it ever was.

During transition, you should address the level of indebtedness against your principal residence. Is it higher than you can comfortably support on your expected level of retirement income? Potential reasons for this are: you traded up to a more expensive home for lifestyle reasons; you took out home equity loans to remodel; to purchase cars; to pay medical bills; or to pay for college or wedding costs for your children. Your goal in the 4th quarter time frame is to increase home equity by decreasing debt levels. In some cases, this may include a decision to trade down in price, size, carrying costs, etc. of your home in order to achieve an affordable monthly cost of housing.

Since your taxable income and marginal income tax rate will likely decrease as you transition into the fourth quarter of life, the tax benefits of home ownership (mortgage interest and property tax deductions) will become less valuable. This means that your after-tax cost of

Tax Planning

borrowed money is rising.

Example: if you pay $10,000 of deductible mortgage interest on a 7.25% mortgage loan, and your taxable income puts you in the 35% federal income tax bracket, your net after-tax cost for that borrowed money is only 4.71% (65% x 7.25% = 4.71%). However, if your taxable income decreases so that you now are in the 25% marginal federal income tax bracket, your net after-tax cost for the borrowed money is now 5.44% (75% x 7.25% = 5.44%).

To reduce the financial tension of mortgage payments in retirement, during the transition period you should focus on both building your retirement assets and reducing the principal balance of any mortgage or home equity loans. Also, during this period, you need to work on converting any variable-rate indebtedness to fixed-rate indebtedness to limit the potential damage of rising interest rates during retirement. If you wait until after retirement to try to do this, you may find it more difficult to qualify for new loans, or you may have to pay higher interest rates on new loans due to your decreased income level.

The federal government's reaction to the 2008 national Financial Crisis has been to take action to reduce mortgage interest rates dramatically in hopes of stimulating increased home sales. At the time this chapter was written, mortgage rates were at historic 50 year lows. This is an excellent opportunity for Baby Boomers with high or variable rate mortgage or home equity debt to refinance to low, fixed rate terms. Try to borrow at the shortest duration possible (10 or 15 year mortgages if you can afford the monthly payments) so that you can reduce the principal balance owed as quickly as possible. An optimum goal is to try to match the mortgage payment term to your anticipated retirement date, so you can retire without a monthly mortgage payment. This is the plan I am following personally.

Note that I am making an assumption that the readers of this book are not carrying any non-tax deductible personal debt at this time, only indebtedness on your residence. If you also have automobile loans, credit card debt or other personal loans, you probably should work to pay these off first and then turn your attention to the indebtedness on your residence.

Sale of Residence Issues

During transition, as you move through the empty-nest syndrome and begin to set your sights on retirement, it is important to consider how to take advantage of the tax benefits available upon sale of your primary residence. Current law allows a married couple to exclude from taxation up to $500,000 of gain on the sale of a residence if it has been owned and occupied by the taxpayers as a primary residence for at least two of the five years prior to the sale date. The exclusion amount is $250,000 for single taxpayers. This exclusion can be claimed multiple times, so long as two years elapse between sales.

This is a black and white rule which offers some planning opportunities, especially for those with multiple residences. For example, suppose you own two residences—your long-time family home in Illinois and a vacation property in Florida, and there is substantial appreciation in both properties. Your goals are: to sell the Illinois home which is now too big, then buy a smaller house nearby (close to the kids and grandkids); then sell the Florida property and buy something else in Florida (same size or larger) to serve as your primary retirement residence.

Tax Planning

In this scenario, the recommended tax strategy would be to sell the Illinois home first since you have used it as your primary residence for two of the past five years. You can go ahead and purchase a smaller property near the kids, but for at least the next two years, you should try to make the Florida vacation property your primary residence by spending more than half the year there, and take other actions evidencing a change in residency from Illinois to Florida (definitely seek advice from a qualified tax professional on how to document this properly).

If done properly, you can use another $500,000 of gain exclusion when you sell the former Florida vacation property in order to purchase the permanent Florida residence. This plan will save capital gain taxes on up to $500,000 of appreciated value in both the first and second properties. Note that losses suffered on the sale of a residence or personal use property (i.e. second home) are not tax deductible.

This strategy can also work for those who own residential rental properties, in addition to their primary residence. If you and your spouse can agree to live in the rental properties as your principal residence one at a time for two years each prior to sale, you can potentially take advantage of the sale of residence exclusion multiple times. Note that a change in federal tax law effective 1/1/2009 reduces the benefit of this opportunity, but only partially. Seek qualified tax advice to fully understand the potential outcome before acting.

Note that there is no requirement to reinvest the sales proceeds into another primary residence. So, if you will move from a high-cost area to a low-cost area at retirement, the $500,000 exclusion may allow you to add to your personal savings, or to reduce or eliminate your mortgage/home equity indebtedness when you purchase a new home. You can even sell your primary residence, keep the proceeds and rent a dwelling instead of making another purchase.

There are special rules related to divorce and remarriage situations, sales of residences owned and occupied for less than two years due to health or other causes, sales following the death of a spouse, and regarding the occupancy period when a taxpayer must move to a long term care facility. The advice of a qualified tax professional will be extremely valuable if you find yourself in one of these situations.

Social Security Benefits

Preparing for the 4th quarter transition can seem like a full-time job when it comes to understanding the complexities of our nation's Social Security benefits. There are at least three distinct aspects of Social Security that you should consider as you prepare for retirement—retirement benefit amounts, earnings limits and taxation of benefits.

With regard to benefit amounts, the Social Security Administration (SSA) sends each adult who pays premiums into the Social Security system an annual statement (your Social Security Statement) shortly before his birthdate. The statement contains your lifetime earnings record reported to SSA by employers and the anticipated retirement benefit amount you should receive if your earnings continue at the present level up to the date you begin taking benefits. The retirement benefit estimates are expressed as a monthly payment amount from SSA—beginning either at age 62 (early retirement), at full retirement age, or at age 70. The longer retirement is deferred, the greater the monthly retirement benefit amount will be. Choosing the best age to

Tax Planning

begin receiving SSA retirement benefits depends on many factors, such as overall health, desire to continue working past age 62, spouse's age and working status, etc. Please review information on the SSA website (www.socialsecurity.gov) or seek assistance from knowledgeable experts in this area before filing a claim for benefits.

One significant factor in determining the best age to apply for Social Security retirement benefits is the effect of the SSA earnings limitation. In a nutshell, this rule acts to reduce or deny benefits to otherwise qualified recipients who continue working. Under current law, if you are below full retirement age (example: full retirement age is 66 years for those born between 1943 and 1954) and receiving SSA retirement benefits, then your earned income should not exceed $14,160 (2009 limit). If it does, your Social Security benefit will be reduced by $1 for every $2 of earned income exceeding this level. Note that earned income includes wages, bonuses, commissions and net profit from self-employment, but it does not include income from pensions, annuities, investments, etc. There is a retirement earnings calculator on the SSA website (www.socialsecurity.gov/OACT/COLA/RTeffect.html) that can help with understanding the effect of this rule. If you will be subject to this rule, it may be worthwhile to delay your application for retirement benefits—as late as the year you reach full retirement age. Once you reach full retirement age, the earnings limitation rules no longer apply.

Finally, the third factor to consider when evaluating your SSA retirement benefit is the applicability of federal (and potentially state) income taxes on the benefit amount. State taxes are too varied to be covered in this book. Under current federal tax rules, when the sum of your modified adjusted

The Transition

gross income plus 50% of your Social Security benefit amount (called "provisional income") exceeds a certain base amount, some of your Social Security benefits will be taxable by the IRS. Modified adjusted gross income is basically your adjusted gross income from your tax return plus any tax exempt interest you earned that year. For 2009, the base amount is $25,000 for a single taxpayer and $32,000 for married taxpayers. Note that the maximum amount of Social Security retirement benefits that can be taxed by the IRS under this rule is limited to 85% of the amount you received from SSA—no matter how high your provisional income goes. So, if your provisional income will exceed these levels in years that you receive SSA retirement benefits, you may benefit by doing some tax/financial planning with regard to your overall income situation. If you won't be able to bring provisional income below the base amount, be prepared for the tax impact on your annual tax return.

State Taxation of Retirement Income

Starting to think about the transition to retirement? For many people, this may include a decision on moving their principal residence to a new state. Taxes should be one of the factors involved in this decision process; however, income taxes are only part of the equation. It is equally important to understand real estate and sales tax burdens in the states on your short list to appreciate the full tax picture. Many states offer tax exclusions or exemptions for seniors in one or more of these areas, which can complicate the analysis. In a recent posting on the website MSN Money, titled "Which States Give Retirees the Best Deal?"(http://moneycentral.msn.com/articles/retire/basics/9

Tax Planning

838asp), the surprising results indicated that a fictional retired couple would suffer the lowest total annual tax burden (income, real estate and sales taxes combined) in Dover, Delaware. Only Nevada made the top 10 for low taxes among states considered retiree tax havens. Surprisingly, Arizona and Florida – perennial retirement meccas – were in the middle of the pack in terms of total tax cost. Sunshine apparently isn't free!

Note that if you do move from a state where you have lived and worked for a long period of time to a new state for retirement, the old state cannot continue to tax your pension income once you are resident in the new state. Withholding of old state income tax from your pension should be canceled. A federal law enacted in 1996 protects retirees from this kind of "long arm" taxation by the former state. However, your new state is permitted to tax the pension income – so be sure to consider this in your planning.

Watching Marginal Tax Rates

It is useful to understand the changes that retirement will have on your effective and marginal income tax rates. For most Baby Boomers, the transition means that their income and applicable tax rates will be decreasing. One result of this change (as mentioned earlier in this chapter) is that the after-tax cost of mortgage interest increases. Other consequences should also be considered.

For example, investments in municipal bonds in taxable accounts may have made sense while you were at the top marginal federal and state income tax rates. However, these investments will lose their luster when your taxable income drops due to your transition. The effect of a decrease in

The Transition

your marginal tax rate on municipal bond investments is that the after-tax yield decreases. As a consequence, the after-tax yield on fixed income investments producing taxable income (i.e. CD's, US Treasury bonds, corporate bonds, etc.) may now be more attractive.

Similarly, special low tax rates on qualified dividends and long-term capital gains should be analyzed to determine how attractive these types of investments and income remain post-transition. When the percentage difference between ordinary tax rates and these special tax rates decreases, the after-tax return on investments producing this tax-favored type of income vs. taxable interest, non-qualified dividends or short-term capital gains could change. Note that the current special low rates are scheduled to expire after 12/31/2010.

The analysis of special tax rates on qualified dividends and long-term capital gains should also include an understanding of the extremely favorable 0% Federal tax rate available beginning in 2008 (through 2010 under current law) for those taxpayers whose incomes do not exceed a certain threshold. For taxpayers in this category, there is an added planning opportunity to receive gifts of appreciated property from family members in higher tax brackets and realize the dividends or capital gain at the lowest possible tax rate. Consult an expert tax advisor for guidance on these possibilities.

Charitable Giving

Individuals embarking on the transition process should consider the manner in which they will make charitable contributions in future years. There are a number of tax planning points to evaluate in this regard. First, if income

Tax Planning

will drop substantially in retirement, the possibility of making a gift (or gifts) to a donor-advised fund prior to retiring should be considered. In this way, the charitable contribution deduction can be accelerated into the current year, at a higher marginal tax rate, and the work to identify suitable charities and make gifts to them can be done in later years when there is more time to invest yourself in the effort.

Second, during retirement an individual may find that they hold substantially appreciated stock or securities following long years of investing. It is important to consider the benefits of donating appreciated stock instead of cash if you plan on making gifts of larger amounts. By doing so, you receive a charitable contribution deduction based on fair market value of the stock, but there is no capital gains tax to pay. The charity doesn't pay tax when it sells the stock either. This is a better result tax-wise than selling stock and using the cash proceeds to make the gift. Consider this for large one-time gifts as well as annual pledge gifts, such as to your church, exceeding $2,000.

Third, you may also find that, when moving from the long-time family home to a smaller residence suitable for empty-nesters, you have a lot of furniture and other personal property to donate to charity. Please be aware that if you make a gift of property valued (at current market value, not original purchase price) at over $5,000, you must obtain an appraisal by an independent appraiser in order to claim a charitable contribution of greater than $5,000.

Finally, be aware that if you enter retirement with no outstanding mortgage on your primary or second residence (congratulations!), the tax benefit of charitable deductions may change dramatically. This is due to the fact that it may no longer benefit you to itemize your deductions, and you may start claiming the standard deduction instead. For

The Transition

2009, the standard deduction for a married couple where both spouses are age 65 or older is $13,600. If your itemized deductions in that year, including state and local taxes, charitable contributions, etc., are not greater than $13,600, you will claim the standard deduction instead. Thus, you will receive no tax benefit for the charitable donations you made. They are truly charitable donations in this situation!

Tax Planning

Funding 529 Plans for Grandchildren

Many people in the midst of transition and in their retirement years would like to assist with the education of their children, grandchildren or great-grandchildren. One very effective way to do this is to make gifts to either a Coverdell Education Savings Account (CESA) or a 529 Plan account for their descendants. Gifts to CESAs are limited in amount (currently $2,000 per year, subject to income limits applicable to the donor) and the beneficiary must be less than age 18; but the attraction is that the funds can be used for education at any age, from kindergarten to post-graduate school.

Gifts to 529 Plan accounts are specifically for college or post-graduate education, and such accounts have much higher contribution limits: up to $65,000 (2009 limit) in one year from each grandparent, with lifetime maximum contribution limits as well. The tax planning idea is to consider opening and funding 529 Plan accounts with the financial provider in your state of residence if they grant a state income tax deduction for such gifts. Generally, there is no requirement that the beneficiary attend a college or university in your state in order to use the benefits.

The Transition

WILLIAM R. GOUGÉR, J.D., C.P.A.
Gougér Franzmann & Hooke, LLC
400 Inverness Parkway, Suite 250
Englewood, Colorado 80112
(720) 266-1040 ▫ (720) 266-1041 fax
www.GFHLawfirm.com

Bill Gougér co-founded Gougér Franzmann & Hooke, LLC in early 1998 with a desire to integrate tax and legal services into one firm so that clients received overall advice without consulting multiple advisors.

He graduated from the University of New Hampshire with a B.S. in Environmental Science (magna cum laude) and received his J.D. from Suffolk University Law School with Honors. He worked in the Tax Department of Ernst & Young for eight years in their Portland, Oregon and Amsterdam, Netherlands offices.

In 1991, Bill came to Colorado to become Tax Director of Echo Star Communications Corporation and was involved in numerous significant corporate transactions.

Bill maintains his professional status as both an attorney and a CPA in the State of Colorado. He is authorized to appear before the Colorado Supreme Court and the United States Tax Court. Bill also is head of the firm's Taxation Practice which renders services to clients regarding tax planning and compliance, conservation easements, stock option planning, high net worth family issues, and tax aspects of financial planning decisions.

Chapter Ten
Estate Planning

By Michael Franzman, J.D., L.L.M., C.P.A.

Estate Planning Section

It is ironic that intelligent people about to transition into the 4th quarter of life think nothing of devoting a great deal of time and financial resources to reducing their income tax burden, yet will invest very little or no thought into the proper planning of their estates. This is peculiar given that the federal estate tax may result in nearly one-half of one's entire life savings passing to the government upon his death. Aside from taxes, the failure to properly plan one's estate can lead to arguments between children that may never fully heal, the distribution of substantial assets to beneficiaries who are not emotionally or financially prepared to deal with them, the loss or failure of

The Transition

family businesses, and other serious problems.

The failure to handle this important area doesn't always stem from simple procrastination. Individuals may sense, often correctly, that the process will be time consuming, expensive, and may touch upon very sensitive topics which are emotionally difficult to think about, let alone discuss. For others, preparing an estate plan may be an admission that they are getting older. While it is very common for couples to make wills when their children arrive, many of these will have not been updated even as the children are now grown and the couple is transitioning into the 4th quarter. It is equally common that couples who already are in the 4th quarter have done no planning at all.

If one has not updated his estate plan in a number of years, it is a certainty that the family situation has changed. The children are now grown, having fulfilled the parents' hopes or perhaps having disappointed. Parents may have passed away or developed an urgent financial or medical need. Perhaps the couple has found their marriage to be more fragile than once believed, or maybe an even stronger bond has been found through the arrival of grandchildren. Any one of these factors is certain to impact how one views his estate.

It is just as certain that the couple's financial situation has evolved. Possibly the couple's net worth far exceeds even what could have been envisioned when they planned their wedding years ago. Real estate prices may have risen to unthinkable heights, only to be suddenly washed away. Others may find themselves holding significant retirement accounts or large amounts of life insurance. Almost always, the sum of the estate comes as a surprise.

Finally, it is a certainty that the laws have changed. While the laws of wills and trusts generally change at a glacial pace, tax laws literally change daily and radical

Estate Planning

changes in the tax code occur over the course of years, not decades. Estate planning methods and options also improve and change over time. Difficult issues that were never fully or satisfactorily addressed in an older estate plan may be resolved by the application of newer techniques or options.

When one begins planning his estate, much of the initial complexity arises from the fact that there are several moving parts that somehow must all be puzzled together. Tax concerns must be balanced against property distribution plans. Concerns about probate avoidance must be weighed against complexities regarding how various assets are titled. Asset protection must somehow strike a balance with providing flexibility to beneficiaries. Then there is the matter of who will carry out the plan as trustee, personal representative, agent under a power of attorney, etc. It is important to engage an advisor who understands these complexities and who can clearly explain them to you.

Transfer Tax System

No matter the size of one's estate, a basic understanding of the applicable state and federal transfer tax system is always a useful starting point. There is no escaping the fact that the desire to minimize transfer taxes drives much of the planning. Nevertheless, a word of caution is in order: you should not allow the tax tail to wag the dog. An estate plan that is very tax efficient but that does not fulfill the basic goals of how and to whom one's assets are to be distributed is not a good plan. It is helpful to consider how you would like your assets distributed if there were no transfer taxes and then allow your attorney the flexibility to draft the plan in the most tax efficient way possible, while still accomplishing your goals.

The Transition

Overview of Transfer Tax System

There are many different taxes that we are called upon to pay as we go through life. Federal and state taxes are levied on income earned by individuals and entities. Sales taxes are levied when we purchase certain goods. Property taxes are levied on property owners based upon the value of real estate and personal property owned. As if this weren't enough, the transfer tax system imposes a tax on certain transfers of property to others.

State transfer tax systems work largely the same as the federal system, so the estate planning techniques to deal with the potential tax liability are similar. Because of this similarity, the following discussion will largely focus on the federal transfer tax system.

There are three separate federal transfer taxes that must be addressed. The first is the federal estate tax. The estate tax imposes a tax on the transfer of assets that occurs as the result of one's death. The other two taxes are the federal gift tax that imposes a tax on the transferor of assets made during one's lifetime, and the federal generation skipping transfer tax that imposes a tax on the transfer of assets to individuals who are more than one generation removed from the person making the transfer.

<u>How is the Federal Estate Tax Calculated?</u> In general, the federal estate tax is imposed on transfers occurring at death that have an aggregate value of more than $3.5 million.

To calculate the tax due, a determination must be made of the value of all assets owned by the decedent. The IRS takes a very broad view of what is considered an asset. This view includes all the obvious assets that one would expect such as bank and brokerage accounts, retirement plans such

Estate Planning

as IRAs and 401(k)s, real estate and ownership in entities such as stock in a corporation or a membership interest in a limited liability company. In addition to the more obvious assets, the gross estate also includes several assets that might not initially come to mind, such as life insurance proceeds and, in some cases, even includes property that was given away by the decedent during his or her lifetime that otherwise escaped the gift tax.

Determination of the value of the assets is merely the starting point in determining the amount of tax due. The decedent's estate is entitled to several important deductions in determining how much tax is actually due.

First, any property that is left to the decedent's surviving spouse, provided the surviving spouse is a U.S. citizen, is deductible in an unlimited amount. Accordingly, if one dies and decides to leave all of his assets to his surviving spouse, there is no tax due upon death. It is important to note, however, that the marital deduction merely serves as a deferral technique and it does not result in the permanent elimination of an estate tax. That is to say, when the surviving spouse subsequently passes away, assuming that he or she has not remarried or consumed all of the assets, a tax may be due. When it comes to paying taxes, later is usually better than sooner, and deferral can be an important and valuable result.

In addition to the unlimited marital deduction, any property that the decedent leaves to a qualified charity is deductible in calculating the amount of estate tax due. Unlike the marital deduction, property that is left to a qualified charity permanently eliminates the estate tax and does not result in a mere deferral of estate taxes.

Next, the decedent's estate is also entitled to deduct administrative expenses. These are typically items such as funeral expenses, expenses of the last illness, legal and accounting fees, etc. Again, the concept is that the taxes are imposed on transfer of assets from the estate to the beneficiaries. Assets that are consumed in making such transfer should rightfully not result in a tax being imposed.

Finally, there is a flat deduction that is available in calculating the estate tax due which is currently $3.5 million per decedent. This amount has changed frequently in recent years and it is important to consult with an estate planning attorney before relying on this amount. Absent future congressional legislation, this flat amount will become an unlimited deduction in 2010 (the oft-discussed repeal of the "death tax"), and then will decrease to $1.0 million per decedent in 2011 and all subsequent years.

The estate tax is essentially calculated by subtracting the deductions described above from the total value of the assets owned by the decedent at death. This difference is multiplied by the tax rate (currently 45%) to determine the tax due. The tax is due within nine months from the date of the decedent's death.

<u>What is the Federal Gift Tax and how is it Calculated?</u>
After enacting the federal estate tax in 1916, Congress realized that it had a significant problem. The estate tax was easy to circumvent provided taxpayers were willing to simply give their assets away prior to death. To correct this problem, the federal gift tax was enacted in 1932.

The federal gift tax is imposed on gratuitous lifetime transfers of property. The tax is imposed on the person who makes the gift rather than the person who receives it. The tax rates for lifetime gifts are the same as those of decedent's estates, that is, the current rate of 45% of the value of the gift.

Many transfers are exempt from the gift tax altogether and two important deductions are applied in calculating

Estate Planning

how much tax is due. There is an annual exemption amount of $13,000, exemptions for payments of qualified educational and medical expenses, a lifetime exemption amount of $1.0 million, and an unlimited deduction for gifts to qualified charities and to our spouses, provided they are a U.S. citizen.

The annual exemption amount permits individuals to transfer up to $13,000 per recipient each year without triggering a gift tax. There are no limitations on the number of recipients and the recipients do not have to be related to the person making the gift. A married couple can elect to gift split, meaning that a married couple can give up to $26,000 per recipient annually irrespective of whether the gifted property actually comes from the husband or the wife. If a couple elects to gift split, a Form 709 must be filed with the IRS.

Example: On December 31, 2009, a wife gives $26,000 to her two children from her individually-owned checking account. On January 3, 2010, she gives her friend $13,000 from the same account. No tax is due on either of these transfers; however, the couple is required to report the 2009 gift with the IRS.

In general, the lifetime exemption permits individuals to gift up to $1.0 million worth of property during their lifetime, exclusive of the annual exemption and the unlimited marital deduction. However, use of lifetime exemption proportionately reduces the amount that can pass free of the estate tax on our death. In other words, we currently can transfer $3.5 million upon our death if we didn't make use of the $1.0 million gift exemption; or, we can leave $2.5 million to our heirs upon our death if we made lifetime gifts totaling $1.0 million.

Most of us rarely analyze the gift tax implications of transfers of property, and to a large extent, our gifts are

The Transition

covered by the exemptions and deductions in calculating if a gift tax is due. The problems generally arise when we begin to change the title on assets to accommodate concerns related to our incapacity, or are trying to pass property to desired beneficiaries while we are still alive. Naming or adding a child or other non-spouse individuals as owner or co-owner of an account, real estate or other asset, instead of properly preparing your estate plan, needlessly risks those assets to gift tax and provides a false sense of preparedness in the event of your incapacity or death.

What Estate Planning Documents do I need?

An estate plan is more than a compilation of documents. An estate plan must analyze the ownership and the beneficiary designations on your assets. This asset titling process is essential to the effectiveness of your estate plan. For example, if you name a beneficiary of your life insurance or co-own property as "joint tenants," then those assets are not controlled by your will or trust. They simply pass to the surviving co-owner or beneficiary automatically upon your death. All of the tax and inheritance provisions contained within your documents for the orderly and efficient disposition of your affairs will not control this property, regardless of whether you make a will or a trust.

A well thought-out estate plan will provide legal analysis and recommendations for your asset titling and, at a minimum, include the following documents:

- Revocable Trust Agreement, Will or Both
- Financial Durable Power of Attorney
- Healthcare Durable Power of Attorney
- Living Will

Estate Planning

- Personal Property Memorandum
- Authorization for Release of Protected Health Information

Revocable Trust versus Will

One of the fundamental questions that you will need to answer is whether to use a revocable trust agreement or a will to dispose of your assets. A revocable trust is often referred to as a will substitute because it accomplishes everything that a will does and more.

A will is an instrument that directs how your assets are to be distributed upon your death. It further sets forth the person or entity that will be in charge of administering your estate after your death. In your will, you may also nominate the person that you would like to serve as guardian of your minor children upon your death.

A revocable trust is a legal document that directs how your assets are to be administered upon either your death or incapacity. It is helpful to think of a trust as a shoebox that holds all of your assets. On the top of the shoebox, there are instructions on how the assets inside are to be managed if you die or become incapacitated. When such circumstances arise, your successor trustee simply takes control of the shoebox and follows its instructions, without the need to gather control of the assets through the use of a power of attorney or through court-controlled conservatorship proceedings.

It is important for you to understand the distinctions between the instruments, and the advantages and disadvantages of each. The following chart highlights some of the similarities and differences between revocable trusts and wills, and also sets out some of the advantages and disadvantages of each.

The Transition

	Revocable Trust	**Will**
Distribution of Assets	Assets are distributed to your beneficiaries based upon the terms of the trust agreement.	Assets are distributed to your beneficiaries based upon the terms of the will.
Estate Tax Savings	If prepared correctly, a revocable trust can reduce the amount of estate tax that you might otherwise have to pay.	If prepared correctly, a will can reduce the amount of estate tax that you might otherwise have to pay.
Effect of Incapacity	Trust assets continue to be managed for your benefit in the event of your incapacity.	A will does not help asset management in the event of your incapacity. A general durable power of attorney is required.
Probate	May result in complete probate avoidance.	Requires probate.
Asset Titling	Requires that assets be retitled into the trust.	No asset retitling is required, but it may be necessary to retitle assets between spouses to achieve estate tax savings.
Out of state assets	Assets located outside of the state of residence are usually	Assets located out of state may be required to be

Estate Planning

	retitled into the revocable trust to avoid ancillary probate.	probated. May result in high administration costs.
Fiduciaries	Trust administered by one or more trustees.	Will be administered by personal representative.
Privacy	Better privacy protection. Does not become a public document.	Becomes a public document when logged with court.
Expense	Generally more expensive to prepare, and less expensive to administer on death or incapacity.	Generally less expensive to prepare, and more expensive to administer on death or incapacity.

Financial Durable Power of Attorney

A financial durable power of attorney, also called a general durable power of attorney, is a document that allows you to designate another person to make financial decisions on your behalf in the event that you are unable to make informed decisions regarding your property.

Having your assets inside of a revocable trust may obviate the need for a financial power of attorney because your trustee will have authority to manage assets inside the trust if you become incapacitated. It is generally good practice to have a general durable power of attorney even if your assets are in a revocable trust. After all, there is the possibility that assets were inadvertently left out of the trust or assets acquired after the establishment of the trust are not properly retitled into the trust.

Healthcare Durable Power of Attorney

A healthcare durable power of attorney, also called a medical power of attorney, is a document that enables you to designate another to make decisions on your behalf in the event that you are unable to make informed choices about your own personal care.

These decisions might include what hospital you are admitted to, who has access to your medical records, whether you permit your agent to relocate you outside of your home state for medical treatment, whether you permit your agent to commit you for an admission to hospice or nursing care and other important matters.

A well-drafted healthcare power of attorney may also include language concerning:

- Whether you permit your agent to commit you for medical treatment against your voluntary wishes; for example, if your agent believed that you were suffering from a mental infirmity
- Your preference for being kept in your personal residence as long as possible for medical treatment before being moved into a care or treatment facility
- Your preference for being an organ donor

Living Will

A living will, not to be confused with the term living (revocable) trust, is an instrument in which you make

Estate Planning

known your wishes concerning the administration of life-sustaining medical procedures.

Essentially the document states that life sustaining procedures will be withheld or discontinued if you have a serious injury, disease or illness which is not curable or reversible; if you cannot communicate medical decisions on your own behalf; and if one or more physicians have determined that the administration of life-sustaining procedures will only serve to postpone the moment of death.

An important distinction exists between a living will and a healthcare power of attorney in that you do not appoint another to make decisions for you in a living will: you are simply making a declaration as to what actions you would like taken or withheld in the event that the circumstances described above exist. There is, however, some potential overlap between the living will and the healthcare power of attorney in that the individual you designate under your healthcare power of attorney may want to take action that is contrary to your instructions under your living will. For example, your agent may be holding on to hope for a miracle cure and feel that life support should be continued, despite what you have expressed in your living will. To minimize the conflict in this situation, it is important to reconcile in advance whether your agent has final authority with respect to life-sustaining treatment or whether your declaration under your living will is the final voice on the outcome.

Two opinions often emerge when this topic is discussed. One viewpoint is a fear of prolonged medical care when all hope is lost or not wanting to put someone in the position to make a decision on another's life. The other viewpoint is a fear of being locked into an inflexible document and an impersonal medical system and the possibility, no matter how small, that the medical situation may improve.

The Transition

Again, it is critical to discuss the matter with your family and agent in order to make your wishes and beliefs known. It is also important to discuss the matter with your physician and to provide them with your executed medical documents in advance.

Personal Property Memorandum

A personal property memorandum is a document that allows you to designate the people who will receive specific items of tangible personal property upon your death; the concept is that you do not need to pay an attorney to revise your will or trust every time you have a change of heart as to who gets the candlesticks.

This list may prove very important in reducing hurt and hard feelings among children who have grown attached to a particular item. Interestingly, it is rarely the financial assets that cause trouble among children. After all, it is easy to divide an account equally among the survivors if that is what is desired. It is often a disagreement over a one-of-a-kind sentimental item that, regardless of value, can irreparably shatter the peace between surviving family members. Be cautious about thinking that this could not happen in your family. Remember the estate planner's adage that you do not really know someone until you have shared an inheritance with them. Prepare your list and keep it updated.

Authorization for Release of Protected Health Information

Congress passed a law entitled the Health Insurance Portability and Accountability act (HIPPA) that limits the use, disclosure or release of individually identifiable health information. A HIPPA authorization is a document that

Estate Planning

establishes who are your Authorized Recipients for health care disclosure under the Standards for Privacy of Individually Identifiable Health Care Information regulations under HIPPA.

Other Fiduciaries

The Personal Representative or Executor is generally responsible for the administration of the decedent's estate. The personal representative's duties may include submitting the will and accompanying documentation to the probate court, safeguarding and collecting assets of the estate, paying pending bills, attending to federal and state income tax matters, making certain distributions to, and setting the expectations of, the beneficiaries, engaging and working with attorneys and accountants, and even dealing with pets.

The personal representative is nominated in the will. It is often the decision of the person making the will to nominate his or her spouse to serve as the personal representative and to also designate one or more successors to serve in the event that the spouse fails or ceases to serve.

Upon the death, the person designated in the will as personal representative is required to either accept or renounce the appointment with the court. Upon appointment by the court as personal representative, the personal representative will be authorized by the court to conduct business on behalf of the estate.

The trustee is the person or entity who is responsible for holding property on behalf of another. The duties of the trustee include the safeguarding of assets, investing of assets and making distribution decisions.

The Transition

Should I Use an Individual Trustee or a Professional Trustee Such as a Bank or Trust Company?

The answer to this question depends on the situation. Many people are justifiably concerned about fees that will be charged by a professional trustee and are apprehensive of an impersonal relationship between the trustee and the children.

Some families choose to designate a professional trustee to fulfill the investment and administrative duties while concurrently choosing a child or family member to serve in the limited role of making distribution decisions. While this scheme does not automatically insure success and tranquility among the beneficiaries, for some families it may be just the right combination to serve the trust beneficiaries.

How Much do Trustees Charge?

Professional trustees generally are compensated for their services based upon their published fee schedule, which can change over time. Most commonly, annual fees are charged based upon a percentage of the fair market value of assets under management. The fee schedule is often graduated so that the higher the value of assets being managed, the lower the graduated rate. For example, the trustee may charge 1.5% for the first $500,000 worth of assets, 1.15% for the next $500,000 and .75% based upon assets exceeding $1 million. Banks and trust companies are usually willing to negotiate a more favorable fee when the fair market value of assets under management exceeds $2 million. Additional fees are likely to be charged for services provided by the trustee that are not comprised within its normal duties. These may include fees for legal services, tax return preparation and corporate finance or investment banking services.

Individuals who serve as trustees are compensated based on what is provided for in the trust agreement. Agreements are frequently written to provide that the trustee is to receive fair and reasonable compensation for the services rendered as a fiduciary. What is deemed fair and reasonable is most likely dependant on factors such as the amount of time that the trustee devotes in administering the trust and the trustee's experience in dealing with such matters. Some families choose to limit the amount of compensation provided; however, this should be done with caution as it is easy to underestimate the complexity of what the trustee will be called upon to do and the time that will be required to properly perform the function.

Miscellaneous Topics

How much does it Cost to Prepare an Estate Plan?

As you might expect, there is no single answer to this question. Legal fees will depend on a multitude of factors such as where you are located, the value of your estate, where your assets are located, whether you are comfortable with your beneficiaries receiving your property outright or whether a trust will be required to be established, whether either spouse has children from a previous marriage, and whether it is anticipated that an estate tax will be due. Perhaps the most prevalent distinction when comparing legal costs is whether you will receive legal assistance with titling and beneficiary designations. A simple will that requires no tax planning, no asset titling assistance, and doesn't require the creation of any trusts may be as inexpensive as a few hundred dollars, while a plan that

The Transition

minimizes estate tax and establishes one or more trusts for beneficiaries is likely to cost several thousand dollars. For families with significant wealth or for those dealing with complicated assets or beneficiary issues, legal fees can be considerably higher.

Many attorneys are willing to provide a free consultation and quote estate planning work on a flat fee basis. This may be desirable as it eliminates receiving an unpleasant surprise at the end of the process.

Despite the undeniably high up-front costs of creating a well-drafted plan, the potential tax savings and the reduction in estate administration fees, as well as the minimization of family disputes, often more than offsets the cost of preparing an estate plan.

How do I Choose an Estate Planning Attorney?

There are many factors that may be important in choosing your estate planning attorney, and there may be many sources of information that may refer you to an estate planning attorney. You may wish to ask friends, your accountant, your financial advisor, or groups you are affiliated with who they would recommend. You may search the phone book and internet for state bar associations or you may search for local members of national estate planning networks. Regardless of where you start, the following factors and suggested questions are important in finding a good estate planning attorney:

- The professional licenses and qualifications are adequate to your needs. The attorney should be licensed to practice law in the state of your residence, and they should have a network of attorneys with which to cooperate on assets located

Estate Planning

in other states and nations. The attorney should also have errors and omissions insurance coverage. If you are apt to move from state to state, seek an attorney who is a member of a national organization that uses the same style of documents.
- The attorney should provide a free initial consultation, during which meeting they should provide either a flat fee arrangement or an estimate of the total hourly fees. Whether flat fees or hourly fees are preferable is largely governed by the scope of services each fee will cover. Ask for the services provided for the fee, and note whether it includes the asset titling assistance, and if so, how much.
- The attorney should have regular review meetings after the initial plan is in place. Ask what services are provided after the initial plan is completed. Your estate plan should be reviewed regularly every one to two years, and a free review is valuable.

How do I Provide For Children From a Prior Marriage?

One of the most difficult obstacles facing second-marriage couples preparing their estate plan is how the children from a prior marriage influence the plan in the event the step-parent survives the natural parent. The natural parent has a difficult choice to make. If we leave all our property to our surviving spouse, will we, in effect, disinherit our children? There are several common strategies in addressing this issue, and many more options to minimize related concerns, but there is no method to leave everything to our surviving spouse outright and also guarantee our children will receive an inheritance on the death of the surviving spouse.

Every estate planning tool that increases the chance of

The Transition

our children inheriting our property, in some manner, reduces the control the surviving spouse has over the assets when we are the first spouse to die. This is typically done by placing the deceased spouse's assets in trust for the surviving spouse, and the trust may provide assistance to the surviving spouse but only should their other assets be used first. Many other options are available to create a palatable arrangement, but only provided the assets do not pass outright to the surviving spouse.

How Much Should My Children Be Involved?

As you can imagine, this question largely depends upon the relationships in your family. A caring and supportive child may be the ideal successor to handle many of your affairs should you or your spouse not be able to act. However, children can cause problems, intentionally or not, with the orderly creation, implementation and execution of your estate plan. Essentially, your children should be involved as much or as little as you feel is appropriate after consulting with your estate planning attorney. You can be certain that your children have thought about what will happen should you become incapacitated or die, whether or not they actually discuss the issue with you directly.

How Do I Provide My Beneficiaries Protection and Flexibility?

Regardless of whether you have a will or a revocable trust, you may want to establish trusts for the benefit of your intended beneficiaries. These trusts need not spring into existence until your death, and the terms of the beneficiary's trust may be included within your will or revocable trust documents. There are many reasons not to

Estate Planning

give your beneficiaries property outright upon your death. Below is a list of the most common reasons:

- Trusts may provide some protection against a beneficiary's spouse or creditor from reaching the trust assets.
- Trusts may avoid the necessity to establish conservatorships for minor or incapacitated beneficiaries.
- Trusts may be crafted to permit otherwise capable beneficiaries a method to pass property to successive generations in a tax-efficient manner with very little loss of control over the property.
- Trusts can be crafted to provide the beneficiary the option of discontinuing the trust or maintaining it for the reasons above.

The Transition

MICHAEL P. FRANZMANN, J.D., C.P.A., L.L.M.
Gougér Franzmann & Hooke, LLC
400 Inverness Parkway, Suite 250
Englewood, Colorado 80112
(720) 266-1040 ▫ (720) 266-1041 fax
www.GFHLawfirm.com

Michael Franzmann is a co-founder of Gougér Franzmann & Hooke, LLC where he heads the firm's Wealth Transfer group. Mike works extensively with high net worth families throughout Colorado and the United States in developing and maintaining their estate planning structures.

He received a B.S. in accounting from the University of Colorado (1990), J.D. from the University of Denver (1995), and L.L.M. in taxation from New York University (1997). A Denver native, he is licensed in Colorado as an attorney and CPA.

Mike is a frequent lecturer on gift tax, estate tax, and generation skipping transfer tax. His articles have been published in the *Journal of Asset Protection* and *Estate Planning Magazine*. Mike is a member of the Colorado and Denver Bar Associations, and is authorized to practice before the Colorado Supreme Court, the 10th Circuit Court of Appeals, and the United States Tax Court.

Chapter Eleven
What Do I Do Now?

After reading this book, I sincerely hope that you found more than one idea and suggestion that you can use in making your transition into the 4th quarter of your life. I also hope the financial information and advice given steers you in the right direction to protect your assets during this national Financial Crisis. But even more important than utilizing the aids and tools, I hope the information in these pages has left you full of positive anticipation for your future, and, most of all, I want it to have left you with peace of mind.

Everyone – and, more specifically, Baby Boomers – will now understand that the 4th quarter of life is the game-winning quarter. It is no longer a time to sit on the bench. It is the quarter to enjoy with friends and family. It is the

The Transition

moment in time when you can stand tall, at peace within yourself, and say, "What I have done for others has made a great difference."

Transitioning does not happen overnight. If there is one thing I have focused on more than anything else in my consulting years it is, "remember—take one step at a time." Most people try to resolve conflicts and adversity by hitting an instant homerun. So, where do you start?

Transitioning smoothly is going to be one of three things to you. It will be........

1. One of the best things you have ever done for yourself!

2. One of the hardest things you have ever done for yourself!

3. Both!

If you do not take time now to transition smoothly, you may spend the time during the 4th quarter of life feeling regret.

You have worked very hard to get to this point in life. It will now take the same kind of determination to transition into the 4th quarter. It will take work, commitment, self-caring and consideration. What happens tomorrow will be determined by the commitment you make to yourself today. You now have the time and the opportunity to slow down, step back and determine where you have been, where you are and where you want to go.

First, simplify your life. Most of us end up losing our most precious resource – time – by unnecessarily complicating our lives. The purpose of this life is to live it. An important thing to remember is that we get just one

What Do I Do Now?

chance, one life. Years ago, when life was getting too complicated for me, I put in the "Strategy" section of my goals to spend cold winter nights reading books by Emerson and Thoreau. When Thoreau moved into a small cabin on Walden Pond for the purpose of discarding the non-essentials in his life, he demonstrated the value of simplicity.

The second most important ingredient that should be addressed at the beginning of transition is to ask yourself, "What do I enjoy?" It is vital that the goals you are trying to achieve are in harmony with who you really are and not dictated by others.

The next step is to approach the future with a sense of direction, combined with a high degree of flexibility. By being flexible, you allow for changes in your strategies. This allows you to move forward carefully and avoid pitfalls along the way.

As a businessman, I have always followed the adage, "Stopping at third base adds nothing to the score." It is necessary to reach home plate. There is only one way life can truly be lived and that is forward. We look back and cherish yesterday, but we must live today. A typical sign of old age is seniors who talk about the past at the expense of enjoying the present. Many times this results in living in the past. Eventually, because of remembering and discussing failures and mistakes, depression sets in.

Memories are wonderful but not at the expense of the present. A quote that keeps me from dwelling in the past is one I saw posted on an outdoor sign. Early one morning, while driving to work, I stopped to get coffee and headed down the street that led past the Senior Center. My father-in-law had recently passed away and the family, especially his widow, continued to bear the emotional burden of losing and missing him. When a couple spends sixty years

The Transition

together, grief at that loss is overwhelming. We don't want to forget our memories, good or bad, but how do we survive periods of grief? The message on the Senior Center kiosk said it best: "Don't cry because it's over. Smile because it happened." One of the elements that can cripple your progress as you enter the 4th quarter is regret that the other quarters are over. Remember, everything is a function of attitude. We need to change our mindset, smile because it did happen and enjoy the opportunity ahead, knowing the 4th quarter of life is ahead of us.

One of the reasons that past generations regretted the first three quarters were over was that they felt they were being kept out of the 4th, and couldn't keep participating in life as they knew it. Baby Boomers will not accept this philosophy. I said before, "I do not mind getting older so long as I can function in the life that I am used to and can do all the things I am used to doing. Being older is not the problem. Not being able to function and do the things I am used to doing is the problem." As long as we maintain our health, most activities can be continued as before. Yes, we may not want to stay awake so long in the evening and, more than likely, we can't run as fast or as long as before. But the need and desire to do any activity can be as intense as in the previous years of our lives.

One of my favorite fiction writers is Dr. Robert James Waller. Many of you remember Dr. Waller's bestseller, *The Bridges of Madison County*. I was fortunate enough to have him as a college professor and to see him transition from a guitar-playing, long-haired hippie to the dean of a business school at the University of Northern Iowa. One of his follow-up books I also enjoyed was *A Thousand Country Roads*. At the end of this book, his central character Robert Kincaid was transitioning into the 4th quarter of his life. I will never forget the ending when Kincaid, sitting behind

What Do I Do Now?

the steering wheel of his pickup, opens the passenger door, looks at his dog and says, "Jump into the truck and let's drive down all those familiar roads and see what we missed along the way." The 4th quarter of life is beautiful in that it affords us the opportunity to reflect, and to see and do things we may have missed in the earlier years of our lives. We just may have to do things a little differently now than we did before. In his epilogue to *The Bridges of Madison County*, Dr. Waller said it best: "So come twirl the big rope again, maybe not so high and wild as you once did, but still with the hiss and the feel of the circle above you and sun falling through the loop, shadows on the ground where the big rope twirls while it is all getting down to last things, down to one-more-times…"

Early last summer, while I was outlining the Robert Waller story for this chapter, a good friend, Vern Martinez, came to my office to ask a question about a ten-screen cinema complex he was currently under contract to purchase. I had brokered and developed commercial real estate my entire career. But, that summer, I was transitioning from being in commercial real estate to writing this book. Vern, who is 66, has had an interesting life and career. He has done everything from being a marine captain during the Vietnam War to constructing highway tunnels through the Rocky Mountains, and is now renovating security in U.S. embassies around the world.

Approaching my desk, he asked, "What are you up to?" I explained that I was working on a chapter for my book and I read him the quote from *A Thousand Country Roads*, along with the epilogue from *The Bridges of Madison County*. Once I finished, he exclaimed, "Wow!" That is powerful stuff." Then, after a long pause, he looked at me and said, "You know, I have always, since being a little boy, wanted to go to Spain and run with the bulls." I

The Transition

encouraged him, saying, "Well, go do it!" Then Vern said he would have to plan to do it in the future. As he spoke, I realized how often people say this kind of thing but never follow it through. I asked him, "If not now, when will you ever do this?" His reply caught me by surprise when he said, "This summer. Will you come with me?" My immediate reaction was that I might have preferred other options than being chased down the streets of Pamplona by a herd of angry bulls, but I said yes, affirming that, as a Baby Boomer, I would stay in the game and play in the 4th quarter of my life.

    We flew to Europe that summer and, after stops in Munich and Madrid, arrived in Pamplona, Spain. Not wanting to waste any time, we checked into our hotel and decided to make our run the next morning – Friday the Thirteenth! The hotel was located right on the route of the running of the bulls, adjacent to the town square. The hotel was La Perla, where Ernest Hemingway had stayed when he made running with the bulls famous in his book *The Sun Also Rises*. Early the next morning we arrived, two men in their sixties, prepared for the run. Hearing the blast of the starter's gun, the running began and we heard the sound of six angry black bulls coming towards us, their hooves pounding the cobblestone. We outraced the bulls for a while, then took refuge alongside the route's medieval buildings. Our hearts were pumping and our adrenaline was soaring. We smiled at each other, knowing that in facing the ferocious bulls, we had also faced the doubts that existed in our minds about this transition period. It is this doubt, not necessarily the reality, that adversely affects both men and women during this period of change. Webster defines doubt as "Being uncertain or undecided about; being fearful and apprehensive." It is doubt that has to be conquered before one can successfully deal with the tasks

What Do I Do Now?

at hand. Unlike a mid-life crisis where people sometimes act out of character, our running with the bulls was an act of symbolism to remove doubt. There is no excuse for being fearful just because you are transitioning into the 4th quarter of your life.

The 4th quarter transition marks the beginning of a new journey, a new adventure. Fortunately, this time we are able to proceed with more experience, preparing us for any crisis. We will not only survive, we will actually thrive. I've always enjoyed the quote by Aldous Huxley: "Experience is not what happens to a man; it is what a man does with what happens to him."

With all of this experience, we are actually in a position for the first time to achieve something we have desired all our lives – that elusive peace of mind. It is the one thing we always sought that is now within our grasp. There is no better feeling spiritually, emotionally and physically than when you are at peace within yourself. Finding the state of nirvana, while living the life you choose, is the ultimate goal. Peace creates freedom, and freedom is a profound gift. To achieve this peace and freedom, you don't need great wealth, influence or power. Two things are required: that you are not in conflict with yourself and that you are not in conflict with the world around you.

Many years ago I came across a creed that was discovered written above the doorway of a church in Baltimore sometime between 1600 and 1700. I memorized this creed, *Desiderata*, and I have relied on its wisdom throughout both my business career and in my life at times when peace seemed so elusive.

The Transition

DESIDERATA

"Go placidly amid the noise and haste, and remember what peace there may be in silence. As far as possible, without surrender be on good terms with all persons. Speak your truth quietly and clearly; and listen to others, even the dull and ignorant; they too have their story. Avoid loud and aggressive persons; they are vexations to the spirit. If you compare yourself with others, you may become vain and bitter; for always there will be greater and lesser persons than yourself. Enjoy your achievements as well as your plans. Keep interested in your own career, however humble; it is a real possession in the changing fortunes of time. Exercise caution in your business affairs; for the world is full of trickery. But let this not blind you to what virtue there is; many persons strive for high ideals; and everywhere life is full of heroism. Be yourself. Especially do not feign affection. Neither be cynical about love; for in the face of all aridity and disenchantment it is perennial as the grass. Take kindly the counsel of years, gracefully surrender the things of youth. Nurture strength of spirit to shield you in sudden misfortunes. But do not distress yourself with imaginings. Many fears are born to fatigue and loneliness. Beyond a wholesome discipline, be gentle with yourself. You are a child of the universe no less than the trees and the stars; you have the right to be here. And whether or not it is clear to you, no doubt the universe is unfolding as it should. Therefore be at peace with God, whatever you conceive him to be. And whatever your labors and aspirations, in the noisy confusion of life keep peace with your soul. With all its sham, drudgery and broken dreams, it is still a beautiful world. Be careful. Strive to be happy."

What Do I Do Now?

Now, what is the true secret of finding and achieving peace? I feel the really great authors over the course of time have continuously given us the clue. One of these authors is Joseph F. Girzone who wrote *Joshua – A Parable for Today*. Toward the end of the book, Joshua tells a group of people, "My peace comes from *within*. The simplicity of my life reflects what I possess *inside*. The simplicity of your life does not come from within. It is rather an escape from the world around you, a denial of what you have been a part of and hurt by. I have no such problem in my life. I do not let myself be hurt by events, I realize all humanity is in a process of growing and, of necessity, will always be imperfect."

Even more than Emerson and Thoreau, my favorite author has been Napoleon Hill. Hill was the protégé of Andrew Carnegie when he was the head of U. S. Steel. Author Hill wrote many outstanding business books during the course of his life. His works typically included using the catch phrase "grow rich." My favorite book, written when he was in his 80s, was *Grow Rich! With Peace of Mind*. In this book, as with Girzone's book, the constant message was the word "within." Mr. Hill writes, "Every adversity has within it the seed of an equivalent or greater benefit." This has saved me from listening to a lot of worthless chatter and taught me to *hear from within*. Anyone who wants peace of mind should remember those three words – *hear from within*. He continues, "Do not hurt any other person in order that you may succeed. I could have added to my wealth by dishonest means on many an occasion, but I would have lost my peace of mind. When nature takes away youth, she replaces it with wisdom. It is impossible for a young person to possess the accumulated wisdom and experience of a person ripe of age. Think that over before you say old age is a drawback."

The Transition

Most people feel that tomorrow is the unknown of life. I feel that the only unknown is *today*, and tomorrow depends on the decisions of today. One decision we will make today is about finding peace of mind in helping others. The 4th quarter offers us the opportunity to help others, something often avoided up until now. We now have the extra time and/or money to be in a good position to give back to our community, our families and more.

We know from the teachings of our childhood and from the experiences throughout life that helping others is profoundly rewarding. In achieving peace, Napoleon Hill wrote, "Make sure your work and your money benefit someone besides yourself."

I am of German heritage and had the opportunity to live in Germany for a couple of years during my military service. I always enjoyed the following adage: "Das Sind Die Starken ihm Lande Die Mit Tranen in Den Augen Lachen Das Eigene Leid Vergessen Und Anderen Freude Machen." In English, the quote reads, "Those are the strong ones in the land, who with tears in the eyes, can laugh, who can forget their own sorrow and who can make joy for other people."

Throughout my business career, as a commercial real estate broker and developer, I tried to continually do the things that would build a positive business reputation. During the 4th quarter of my life, I have now learned that reputation is about what you do for yourself and legacy is about what you do for others. Legacy does not have to be grandiose. You don't have to be an Abraham Lincoln, whose legacy is the admiration of most Americans. To be loved by your grandchildren is legacy enough.

No matter what your life has been up until now, it is still possible to positively impact your legacy in the 4th quarter of your life. This was brought home to me when I

What Do I Do Now?

watched a great football game between # 1 ranked Ohio State and # 2 ranked Michigan. The star players all were having a terrific game but, toward the end, one of the quarterbacks really began to stand apart from the crowd. The announcer said, "What you do in the 4th quarter dictates what your legacy really is."

I mentioned how the *Desiderata* carried me through many unsettling periods in my life. Now, as I transition, an essay entitled "What Will Matter" by Michael Josephson is what I concentrate on the most.

The Transition

What Will Matter

"Ready or not, someday it will come to an end. There will be no more sunrises, no minutes, hours or days. All the things you collected, whether treasured or forgotten, will pass to someone else. Your wealth, fame and temporal power will shrivel to irrelevance. It will not matter what you owned or what you were owed. Your grudges, resentments, frustrations and jealousies will finally disappear. So, too, your hopes, ambitions, plans, and "to do" lists will expire. The wins and losses that once seemed so important will fade away. It won't matter where you came from, or on what side of the tracks you lived, at the end. It won't matter whether you were beautiful, handsome, or brilliant. Even your gender and skin color will be irrelevant. So what WILL matter? How WILL the value of your days be measured? What WILL matter is not what you bought, but what you built; not what you got, but what you gave. What WILL matter is not your success, but your significance. What WILL matter is not what you learned but what you taught. What WILL matter is every act of integrity, compassion, courage or sacrifice that enriched, empowered or encouraged others to emulate your example. What WILL matter is not your competence, but your character. What WILL matter is not how many people you knew, but how many will feel a lasting loss when you're gone. What WILL matter is not YOUR memories, but the memories that live in those who loved you. What WILL matter is how long you will be remembered, by whom and for what. Living a life that matters doesn't happen by accident, it's not a matter of circumstances but of choice. CHOOSE to live a life that matters."

Journal
Adversity & Perseverance
(My Story About Four Years of Struggle)

January 10, 1989

As I prepare to write my annual goals for 1989, I take a moment to review my favorite quotes regarding keeping a positive mental attitude so I can approach the world with the right frame of mind. At this point, I must give myself a pat on the back for the endurance and strength I have shown over approximately the last 18 months. As I sit here, my mind reviews the negative events which have beaten me down, both mentally and physically.

Never once did I stop, diligently working long hours to correct these negative events. Now I continue, with hope and a prayer, that the future will hold positive changes. It had better, since I am getting close to begging.

The Transition

In the early morning quiet of my office, my mind starts to remember . . . in looking at my real estate business, I wonder how I failed after so many years of meeting projected goals. I begin to blame myself but then read an article about the Savings & Loan Crisis which provides clarity as to what really happened.

In general, the national real estate industry was adversely affected by:

- Deregulation of the Savings & Loan industry

- The Tax Reform Act of 1986

At the same time, in Colorado the real estate industry was adversely affected by two additional conditions:

- An already "overbuilt market condition"

- A migration of people leaving the state because of negative events in the oil and airline industries causing other industries to subsequently exit the state

I have always said, "Business is really about solving problems, and he who does the best wins!" I have also stated, "We all make our own luck and cause our own demise."

Because it is important to never forget and to learn from our experiences, I am now compiling a list of these problems, events and circumstances:

- In 1974, I started my first real estate corporation. In May of 1987, a legal judgment was entered against it in the amount of $95,480. Without my

Journal

knowledge, one of my partners and broker for the firm was involved in a lawsuit for the return of an earnest money deposit on a cancelled sale. He was sued personally and subsequently declared bankruptcy since he could not pay the judgment. The plaintiff then sued the corporation (and me) although we had no knowledge regarding the sales contract. After paying mounting legal fees to defend myself and the company, we ultimately had to close. I then had to start a new real estate company.

- In April 1987, my series of problems began when my partnership's lender, a Savings & Loan in Illinois, refused (for no valid reason) to ratify a sales contract on one of our twin office buildings. The sale of this building would have provided a $250,000 down payment to the partners and would have relieved the partnership of $550,000 in debt (one-half of the total). My commission would have been $35,000 with sale proceeds of $12,650, both of which were desperately needed. Subsequently, the extreme vacancy of the two buildings in the slow Colorado economy caused the partnership the necessity of contributing more than $120,000 in cash for support over the next 20 months. Because of our disagreements with the Savings and Loan, we discontinued making mortgage payments for the next ten months and subsequently had payments in arrears of over $100,000. The savings institution sued us personally for $993,000 and we sued them for Lender Liability. The lawsuits are presently pending and the outcome may not be known for over a year.

The Transition

- In June 1987, the investors who had purchased our shopping center defaulted on their $650,000 promissory note owed to our partnership (the same partnership which owns the office buildings.) My share of this note receivable was $71,500. Since losing the sale of the office building, the partnership was not strong enough financially to take over the shopping center and ultimately had to sell the note receivable for approximately $200,000 cash, losing about $450,000 of future income.

- During the summer of 1987, a partner of mine in another partnership regarding a development parcel decided he did not want to continue with the investment. This investor, an ex-rock star turned born-again Christian and presently a minister in Boulder, had invested $250,000 into this long-term investment project. He sued the partnership to regain his capital, ultimately causing me the necessity of obtaining a new loan for $250,000 to return his cash.

- In the fall of 1987, a Denver real estate firm defaulted on its lease and moved out of a single tenant office building we owned (believe it or not, this was yet another partnership.) Only 12 months before we had invested over $20,000 in renovations to the office space for this firm and there was $48,000 remaining in lease payments. Because of the slow rental market, the space has remained vacant for the last one and a half years.

- In October of 1987, my personal secretary was hospitalized for stress and had to leave her employment for a two-week period. When she

Journal

elected not to return to work, my new secretary discovered that my previous secretary had embezzled over $2,000. Over the next eight-month period, I had to hire four replacement secretaries due to their inadequacies and/or personal problems. This turn-over in personnel was very devastating for my company, creating havoc and not allowing for progress.

- Although an unemployment claim had never been made against my business in over 15 years, I had three claims submitted in the fall of 1988. I protested two of these claims, at a cost of almost $3,000 in attorney's fees. Even though I was justified in both cases, the State ruled against me resulting in my payment of the unemployment claims. In one case, an ex-employee actually made money with a side business while receiving unemployment checks, and in the other case it was my secretary who had embezzled.

- In the spring of 1988, it was discovered that property taxes had not been paid on 640 acres that had been returned to me in a foreclosure. Without my knowledge, the property was sold at a tax sale resulting in the need for me to pay three years' worth of taxes to redeem it. I did not believe this to be a problem since the taxes should have amounted to approximately $860 for the three-year period. Because of a mistake in the County Assessor's Office, the tax amount was mistakenly put into the computer as $22,000. In an effort to correct the mistake, I had to threaten suit against the County. I ultimately won the case, and the County

The Transition

Commissioners agreed to change the taxes to the correct amount. Unfortunately, the State of Colorado is the final authority in making decisions for adjustments regarding taxes because of error. The State reversed the decision and I was forced pay the $22,000 in taxes in order to retain ownership of the property. I am still waiting for my appeal to be heard but to date have waited ten months and still do not have a hearing date.

- Besides conducting my real estate business, I also operated a six-horse Belgian hitch. I had signed a contract with a large meat packing company to represent them at fairs and rodeos. The contract provided a minimum fee of $100,000 on an annual basis. In May of 1988, the General Manager notified me that the contract was to be terminated. As of that date, I had appearances scheduled for the remainder of the year, providing an income to me of approximately $84,000. After the cancellation of the contract and termination of all events, my attorney and I prepared to sue the parent company headquartered out of Chicago. Its attorneys were unaware of my 14-page contract agreement with the Colorado company. When they had instructed the local General Manager to cut expenses for the year, they told me "They did not intend for him to break legal contracts." Due to other financial problems and a lack of liquidity, I decided to settle out of court with the company for $32,500.

- With my hitch contract cancelled and the severity of the negative real estate industry, I had to sell all my horses, hitch equipment and semi truck in order to

Journal

create cash flow.

- In September, a gymnastics studio tenant defaulted on a new building which I had just completed in June of 1988. After three months of occupancy, the tenant moved out of a 6,700 sq. ft. suite leaving me obligated with payments of $4,200 per month and a loan liability of $370,000. I sued the tenant for a personal judgment, but he declared bankruptcy to avoid payment and left me with the obligations.

Due to the list of events I described combined with the negative real estate market, I was left with few sources of revenue. This period ultimately cost me over $187,000 in cash and a decline in net worth of over $500,000.

REVIEW OF 1989

I just paid my income taxes for 1989 which provoked me to think about the journal I wrote in January, 1989. As it is 15 months later, I felt that it important that the events again be made of record as the saga continues:

- During 1989, my problems with the Savings and Loan lender in Illinois became worse. As a matter of fact, they became ridiculous. The good news was that on February 20, we reached a settlement agreement with FSLIC (the regulatory agency for Savings & Loan Banks) which would have ended the suit and the default. The agreement was prepared by their attorney and sent to Chicago for review and signature. The bad news was that the agreement was never signed since FSLIC received information that

The Transition

they were to be taken over by the FDIC on April 6, 1989. The FDIC revoked the settlement agreement and declared it null and void. After one year of legal arguments, the judge granted us a trial to determine the validity of the settlement agreement in January of 1990. After three days of testimony, the judge ruled in favor of the FDIC via Summary Judgment. He did this after closing arguments as the jury deliberated outside of the courtroom. In speaking with the jury after the trial, they explained to my attorney that they felt the government witnesses were incompetent and far from truthful in their testimony. The jury stated that they would have ruled in favor of my partnership. In February, we negotiated a monetary settlement with the FDIC. Believing the judicial process was ended, we submitted our financial statements to the FDIC as part of the settlement agreement. After doing so, the FDIC submitted a 35-page motion to the court seeking a judgment against us for $1,385,000 plus court costs. As of the day of this writing, our personal legal fees have been approximately $90,000.

- Previously I had mentioned that I had granted a Denver commercial bank a Deed in Lieu of Foreclosure on industrial condos I had built as well as on five commercial acres I owned. In having to forfeit the five-acre parcel for equity settlement, I lost approximately $200,000. Also, this resulted in a taxable gain for my 1989 income taxes in the amount of $187,000 because of net loan relief resulting from returning both properties back to the bank.

Journal

At this time, the Colorado real estate economic recession has cost me over $250,000 in cash and a net worth decline of $1,750,000.

REVIEW OF 1990

- On April 14, my CPA advised me that my taxes for the year would be approximately $500 plus the quarterly deposits I had made during the year. On the morning of April 16 he surprised me with a new figure of $5,200 being due and payable.

- On the evening of May 4, 1990 my son Tom (who is in college) had an auto accident which totaled his car and left his passenger hospitalized with a severely broken foot and dental injuries. Tom was charged with D.U.I and vehicular assault. Since these were severe charges which could drastically change a person's life, we hired one of the best attorneys in this field. Thankfully all worked out well in that his passenger was recovering from her injuries quite miraculously and Tom's charges were dropped to a D.W.I with a deferred judgment on the vehicular assault charge.

- When it rains, it pours. On May 23, 1990 the IRS notified me that they wanted to audit me for 1987. Once the audit started, all seemed to be going quite well. When almost completed with the audit, the agent received a request from headquarters to conduct five more audits on me. These audits were for 1987, 1988, and 1989 personally as well as three years' of audits for my corporation. I felt that these audits had been triggered by the FDIC (RTC)

The Transition

lawsuit, but the IRS agent said the audit was targeted by computer because of the large losses declared. Jokingly, the agent stated that the IRS could not determine how a person could lose so much money for three years and still be operating. At the completion of the audits, the IRS has determined that an additional $18,000 was owed. During that period, I had $191,000 of capital gains which was the result of losing properties to the banks. No cash was received from these capital gains. The only real source of cash during this period was from intricate borrowing I had established in order to provide working and living capital. The contention of the IRS (which caused the tax amount due) was that since I had money to operate and live on, I should have treated this money as salary, whereas both my company and I, as an individual, should have paid the appropriate taxes on these earnings. My contention was that there wasn't any money available to pay me a salary and thus I provided funds to myself through the borrowing of money and the sale of properties which provided some return of equity, both of which the IRS usually qualifies as investment income other than ordinary income. They won!

- In September 1990, my $1,073,000 mortgage on a self storage project I had built was due for renewal with United Bank of Denver. During the course of five and a half years, my partner and I had not missed any mortgage payments nor had we been late on any payment. During this rough economic period, we had successfully increased the leasing to a 90% level. The bank called for a new appraisal

Journal

which they stated was just for the file and would not affect the loan renewal. The new appraisal came in at $960,000 which was approximately $116,000 less than the loan amount. Because of this, the bank "classified" the loan. Since they were trying to close a merger with a large national bank they elected to foreclose on the property. In September, I informed the bank I would not pay down nor personally guarantee the $1,075,000. The bank stated they would foreclose and seek a deficiency judgment of approximately $250,000, or I could sign a Deed in Lieu of Foreclosure and give them an extra $100,000 cash. After many negotiations, I gave the bank my 380-SL Mercedes and a promissory note for $25,000.

- In December 1990, I had to sell my ranch, "Sundance Land & Cattle Co." I believe it was Dickens who said, "It was the best of times and it was the worst of times." The sale of the ranch provided me the necessary money to pay the IRS obligations and upcoming payment due the Resolution Trust Corporation for the Plaza Center Buildings. Even though I do not own the ranch any longer, it seemed only fitting that my pride and joy and favorite place on earth provided the necessary cash to bail me out of my severe cash flow problems. Even though I will miss the ranch desperately, my memories will never fade and I always will feel fortunate that I had it for 13 years. In that time period, I created one of the most beautiful ranches in the area and put together one of the best draft horse hitches in the entire United States.

The Transition

REVIEW OF 1991

- Entering into 1991, I knew that the race was coming to an end but the final goal still needed to be met. For three years my goal was to survive and avoid personal bankruptcy. It would have been a much easier road to declare bankruptcy three years earlier but I insisted this was not a legitimate alternative for me. Even though I was very tired, I realized that most races are either won or lost in the last 10 yards. I had to push on.

- In January, I used the cash proceeds from the ranch sale to pay existing debt obligations and to create (protected) cash equities and family funds. I made a payment to the IRS in the approximate amount of $31,000 which made me current in all tax obligations. I then paid my RTC obligation for the second payment due in the amount of $36,450. My next step was to create additional equities for my wife (who had ownership of our house) by paying off the Second Deed of Trust on our residence, in the amount of $165,000. Knowing that cash flow was to be sparse for the next few months, I made advance payments for ongoing obligations such as all insurance policies and property taxes which were due and/or payable in the next six-month period.

- Thinking that I had only one more severe financial problem left, I was quite surprised when on May 4 (the anniversary date of Tom's car accident) I was served with a $750,000 personal liability lawsuit by the injured party in Tom's car accident. The timing of this was quite upsetting to our family since we

Journal

were served just three hours before celebrating my wife's parents' 50th wedding anniversary. Being named a party in this suit was very much of a negative in that it would delay the start of my upward climb towards reorganization of my assets and future income stream.

- The last liability affecting me in 1991 was a debt of $1,400,000 to a Denver Savings & Loan on our shopping center property. If I was not successful in ridding myself of this debt, all my prior work would have been for naught. After extensive negotiations lasting from January through May, success was finally reached on May 28 in deeding the property back to the Savings & Loan without a foreclosure or a deficiency judgment.

It is now my privilege to end this saga which began in May of 1987. A four-year period is much too long to be under constant stress. As this chapter in my life comes to a close, it is one that I will always remember but will never want to repeat.

I thought I knew what success was when I previously experienced all the highs—expensive toys, receiving accolades from others, seeing stories in newsprint regarding my achievements and having the age-old title of "millionaire." Little did I know what was to come next. We all realize life itself is no more than a series of events. Only the experience of living can reveal just how low the valleys and high the mountains actually are.

I have discovered that true success is overcoming life's adversities using our God-given talents. To overcome adversity is a battle which demands a positive focus with a sincere perseverance.

The Transition

During this entire period, I felt I could not reveal my game plan to anyone. In case I did not make it through this period financially, my first goal was to protect my family. I realized that they were being affected emotionally but there was no way to avoid that. Financially, I legally protected them by providing them with over $250,000 of cash and equities (for housing and college). Although I desperately needed these funds during this period, I am proud of the fact that I was able to put the needs of my family first.

My goal was to avoid personal bankruptcy and to also rid myself of real estate properties with severe debt loads. My intuition for the 1990s indicated to me that the ownership of pre-1986 Tax Reform Act properties was analogous to "shooting a dead horse." By ridding myself of all these properties and their corresponding debt, I could now enter the new real estate market without carrying over burdens from the past. By using over $200,000 in cash and intricate business techniques, I convinced lenders to take back properties without foreclosure and deficiency actions, ridding myself of $4,400,000 of debt in a 30-month period. I did lose a net worth of approximately $2,000,000 but I am fortunate not to feel any true loss or anger. At this point in time and at my age (45), I have truly determined that my joy of life comes from the <u>adventure</u> of life itself instead of receiving the blue ribbon.

Dennis Niewoehner